Wide Eyes

Wide Eyes

A War Orphan Unlocks the Mystery of
Her Latvian Roots after Seventy Years

Marija Platace Futchs Fine

Library of Congress Control Number: 2016904084
ISBN: Hardcover   978-1-5144-3701-8
                   Softcover   978-1-5144-3700-1
                   eBook   978-1-5144-3699-8

Print information available on the last page.

Rev. date: 07/18/2016

To order additional copies of this book, contact:
Xlibris
1-888-795-4274
www.Xlibris.com
Orders@Xlibris.com
729520

CONTENTS

For Leonora

GUIDE

Family Names

THERE ARE LATVIAN and Latgalian names for male and female family members. Each language has its own naming conventions. Most Latvian male names end in *s* (Jāzeps, Jānis, Augusts), with occasional names ending in *o* (Otto). Latvian female names can end in either *u* or *a* (such as mine, Marija or Mariju). I also have a patronymic name; I can add *a* to my father's name of Broņislavs, which is Broņislava. My father used my patronymic name a number of times when he searched for me, since he did so in Soviet times.

My mother's name is spelled three different ways in this narrative. Solomeja is the Latvian form of a Polish name. It appears as Solomeija, as well as Salomeja. The Germans spelled it Salomea. Her tombstone shows Solomeja, which is how I use it throughout this memoir.

A woman's married name ends in *e*; hence, my mother's name was Solomeja Platace. As my father's daughter, I have the name Marija Platace. Male surnames end in *s* or *is*, so my father's name is Broņislavs Platacis.

Latgale, the region from which my family comes, has its own language. Names suggest gender as well as case. If the name ends in an *a*, it denotes a female (Platača). However the family name of a female can end in *s*, (Platačs). The *u* ending (Plataču) denotes "family of."

Nicknames end in *a* regardless of gender. Within my family, Malvīna's nickname was Maļa, Ļoņa was Leonora, Broņka was Broņislavs, Vitķa was Vitālijs, and Ģeļa was Helēna.

Platacis Family Names

My family followed the tradition that many other Latvian families used, choosing the same given names for their children. The Platacis clan favored the names of Antons, Andris, and Jānis for boys. Popular girls' names were Malvīna, Helēna, and Leonora.

This fondness for drawing on a limited bank of favorite names continued as grandparents and parents established second families. As a result, I have two Aunt Leonoras (one each on my mother's and father's side), two Helēnas (my grandmother and a cousin), and two Malvīnas (my grandmother and an aunt). I also have two brothers and a nephew named Andris.

The Platacis family tree appears on page xviii, showing only twenty-seven of at least one hundred persons in my family, going back to great-great-great-grandfather Abrams Platacis of Saint Petersburg, Russia. This multigenerational memoir focuses on twelve persons. They include grandfather Augusts; his second wife, Helēna; Augusts's three brothers, Alberts, Antons, and Kazimirs; Augusts's sons, Broņislavs, Vitālijs, and Jāzeps; and his daughters, Leonora and Malvīna. My mother, Solomeja, and my father's son from his second marriage, Andris, round out the remaining cast of characters. The daughters of my great-uncle, Monika and Jānina, come in for special mention in a later chapter.

Three relatives in this narrative are half relatives. Augusts's second wife, Helēna, was my step-grandmother. Their daughter, Leonora, is my half aunt. Andris Platacis, the son of my father's second wife, is my half brother. But to my mind they are all family: grandmother, aunt, and brother. I will refer to them in that way in this narrative.

Alternate Spellings for Other Names

Augusts's name is August when the Polish form of address, *Pan,* is used.
Balts refer to persons from Estonia, Latvia, and Lithuania.
Baltics can refer to the people or to the states they come from.
Dr. Bergfelds is another spelling for Dr. Bergfelde.

MARIJA PLATACE FUTCHS FINE

Rusišku sādža appears as Rusiški village, or as just Rusiški. (The *i* replaces the *u* when sādža is absent.)

Acronyms and Abbreviations

DP	displaced persons
IRO	International Relief Organization
ITS	International Tracing Service (a branch of UNESCO)
LWF	Lutheran World Federation
LWR	Lutheran World Relief
NJLSS	New Jersey Lutheran Social Services
NKVD	The People's Commissariat for Internal Affairs (The Soviet Union's secret police, the predecessor of the KGB)
NLC	National Lutheran Council
UNRRA	United Nations Relief and Rehabilitation Administration

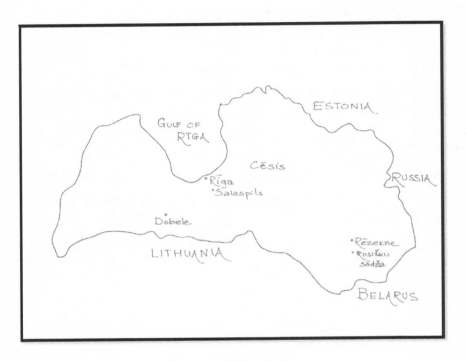

Map of Latvia

Marija Fine 2016

Rusišku sādža, birthplace
Rēzekne, imprisonment
Rīga, orphanage
Salaspils, separation from mother
Dobele, father's home

INTRODUCTION

T HE FIRST SIX years of my life were a mystery waiting to be solved. Mine is a personal story that was buried by the political struggles of World War II. It would take seven decades before I could find out what happened in those years.

In 1949 I came to America at the age of six as a Soviet Latvian war orphan. When I arrived in the United States with seventy-five other Baltic children, my papers gave my name as Marija Platačs. My birth date was May 30, 1943, and my place of birth was Andrupene, Latgale, Latvia. There was no way to verify any of that information. The Cold War between the United States and Russia precluded me from finding out who my birth parents were for half a century.

A clergyman, John Futchs, and his wife, Selma, adopted me. John and Selma were national Lutheran church leaders, both of them serving on national church boards. As a missionary for the Board of World Missions, Selma served as an English teacher at Tokyo Women's Christian University. After her return to the United States in 1941, she edited some national church publications. John Futchs served in parishes in Virginia, Pennsylvania, and Colorado, before becoming bishop of the Rocky Mountain Synod with its headquarters in Denver.

John and Selma worked with John's brother, the Reverend Carl Futchs, to adopt me. Carl was social secretary of New Jersey Social Services, in charge of resettling Latvian refugees. I had stellar parents who urged me to be proud of my Latvian heritage, and at the same time, they helped me take steps to become an American citizen.

They arranged visits with the Latvian orphans I had known in the orphanage in Hahnenklee, Germany. They kept my name, Marija, only changing the *j* to *y* so people would pronounce my name as the Latvians would. They realized that with an unusual name like Mariya, people would ask its origin. They were right. When people heard my name, they would always say, "That is a beautiful name," which opened up the conversation about my being an adopted Latvian orphan.

The one time I did search for information about my Latvian parents was when a college classmate in 1963 asked me to give her any information I might find for an article she was writing on my Latvian roots. I wrote to the mayor of the small town of Hahnenklee. He gave one helpful lead, a lady living in Australia. She was the niece of the director of that orphanage, Dr. Veronika Bergfelds, who also used the alternate spelling of Bergfelde. Ms. Darzins, reporting for her aunt, said she remembered me, Marija Platačs, and that I was from Andrupene, Latgale, Latvia.

She said I was admitted to the orphanage in Riga because there were no known relatives. Although she gave no names for my parents, she recalled that my father was fighting against the communists and my mother died in childbirth. That was the story I gave everyone for the next fifty years.

Once independence returned to Latvia, I resolved to return to the land of my birth, but family matters delayed my going back in the following years. I was the principal caregiver for my husband, Irwin, who battled Alzheimer's disease for fourteen years. After Irwin's death in 2011, the Latvian trip loomed back in view.

That time was 2014. I thought that if I were lucky, I might find the names of my parents on a tombstone or in church records in Latgale. In preparation for my trip, I went to the Latvian Embassy in Washington, DC, where I met Third Secretary Ilze Vituma. I asked her how I could search for the names of my parents. She asked me for my naturalization papers and marriage certificate. She suggested I not raise my hopes, as many records were destroyed during the war.

Two days later she called to say, "I have good news for you. Your father was Broņislavs Platacis, born on January 7, 1919. Your mother

MARIJA PLATACE FUTCHS FINE

was Solomeja Platace, born on September 4, 1920." My heart stopped, and my eyes widened in amazement, being true to my name, as *Platacis* means "wide eyes" in Latvian.

Ms. Vituma found there were fifty families with the name of Platacis in Latvia but that I would have to find the one related to me. Perhaps one gentleman with that name and currently living in Latgale was just that person. She gave me his telephone number, and I entered that number into my mobile phone.

My conversation with Mr. Platacis in Andrupene lasted sixty seconds because he knew no English and I knew no Latvian. That was when I discovered that as one went out from Rīga, there were fewer people who spoke English. I needed to find a guide who could speak Latvian and could begin the search on my parents in advance of my trip.

That person was Lauris Olups, whose name the American Latvian Association in Rockville, Maryland, gave to me. He lived in Riga and worked as a family detective, by researching family origins of overseas Latvians who wanted to return to their native land to meet relatives. I went onto his website, saw that he had already handled a few cases which brought together overseas Latvians with their relatives. I gave him the basic outline of my story, and asked him to help me in my search. His answer was quick and enthusiastic: "Your story is fascinating. I would love to be a part of it."

He became an integral part of the discovery process. He called the man named by my Latvian Embassy official, Mr. Platacis, with whom I had the stumbling sixty-second conversation. He was not related to my family, but he gave names of other people for Lauris to call.

He found his lodestar in Leonora Platace. She remembered me, telling Lauris she was my father's sole surviving sibling. She babysat for me when she was nine years old. The mystery of those first years began to crack open. Now I had a living relative who could link me to the first years of my life. Lauris also found a half brother, whom I would meet along with Aunt Leonora when I visited in August 2014. That person was Andris Platacis, the son of my father's second marriage.

Hundreds of e-mails have gone back and forth between us. This discovery process has stunned me at every turn. Within months I learned Dr. Bergfelde gave the wrong information about my parents. The stories of Solomeja and Broņislavs were to unfold in the most unexpected way as the search continued.

My two locksmiths were Aunt Leonora Platace and Lauris Olups. A half century divides them in age. Each brought their unique perspectives in the search for my family origins.

Leonora, an octogenarian with a steel-trap memory, provided the family lore going back three generations. Because it was oral history, I decided to measure it against the actual record of events. To that end, I drew up a list of questions for Lauris to pose to Leonora and to research in as many resources as possible.

Lauris was a story in himself. Not yet thirty years old, he grew up in an educated family. At an early age, he lost his father, who died in an auto accident. His earliest mentors were his mother, a folklore and literature researcher; and his grandmother, who taught Lauris to read in Latvian and Russian at the age of three.

His restless intellect, combined with his passion for travel and adventure, did not lend themselves to the confines of formal education. He dropped out of high school once and the university twice, during which times he mapped out for himself a curriculum that included readings on philosophy, psychology, and spirituality. He broadened that course of study with field studies that took him on travels inside Latvia or overseas in such diverse countries as Finland and India.

He earned a bachelor's degree in psychology from the Riga Teacher Training and Educational Management Academy (RPIVA) in November 2015, which included the successful presentation of a thesis. He is continuing to study acting and plans to move into psychotherapy or a similar field in the future.

The idea of becoming a family detective grew out of listening to an audiobook, *The Examined Life* by therapist Stephen Grosz. In one chapter, he wrote about a journey he took with his father in Ukraine to visit places of his childhood. He hired a detective/guide to do this.

As Lauris was traveling back home on a tram, he knew it would kill him to "make ends meet in a menial job," so he developed the idea of helping overseas Latvians find or reunite with their relatives. He

MARIJA PLATACE FUTCHS FINE

resolved to start planning how he could make himself a family detective to help overseas Latvians discover or reconnect with their families.

He has published several articles about my story, one of them appearing in *The Baltic Times* in February 2015. He has provided his superior research skills by uncovering original sources such as census records, landowning documents, marriage certificates, even my orphanage record.

He spent hours in libraries and archives and talked with upwards of a dozen people who knew my parents. He used his considerable language skills, translating Russian and Latvian articles germane to my search. My family detective would reveal how my family and I navigated the crossroads of the conflict between the Russians and the Germans.

Lauris Olups
Photo by Uģis Nastevičs, 2014

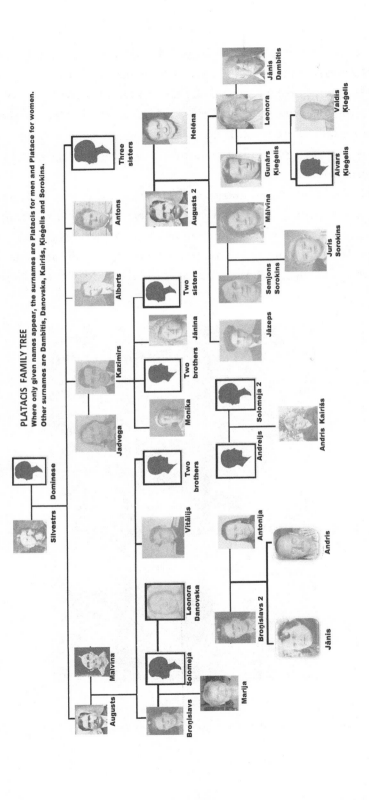

PLATACIS FAMILY TREE

Where only given names appear, the surnames are Platacis for men and Platace for women.
Other surnames are Dambītis, Danovska, Kairišs, Ķieģelis and Sorokins.

Silvestrs — Dominese

Augusts — Malvīna

Jadvega — Antons — Alberts — Kazimirs — Three sisters

Broņislavs — Solomeja — Leonora Danovska — Vitālijs — Two brothers — Monika — Two brothers — Jānina — Two sisters — Augusts 2 — Helēna

Marija — Broņislavs 2 — Antonija — Andrejs — Solomeja 2 — Jāzeps — Semjons Sorokins — Malvīna — Gunārs Ķieģelis — Leonora — Jānis Dambītis

Jānis — Andris — Andris Kairišs — Juris Sorokins — Aivars Ķieģelis — Valdis Ķieģelis

CHAPTER 1

The Arrests

They Won't Take Me!

ON MARCH 13, 1944, Latvian police[1] marched on the snow-covered road from Andrupene to Rusišku sādža[2] to arrest my family for its resistance to the Nazis. Two dozen officers on horseback, some of them hauling wagons, approached our farming community, ready to seize my grandfather, Augusts; father, Broņislavs; his brothers; and half a dozen Soviets.[3]

A Forewarning

The day before, Augusts sensed that an arrest was imminent. His nephew, Antons Galdiņš, warned him that he heard they might be taken into custody by the local quisling police. Antons lived in the same building where Viktors Rukmanis had his office. He was a prominent local Latvian politician and Nazi collaborator who had harassed Augusts for weeks.

Antons overheard a telephone conversation between Rukmanis and, he thought, some German official. Antons told Augusts the words *Platacis* and *arrest* came up in the same sentence.

Rukmanis was someone Augusts had squared off against several times over the refusal of his son, my father, and his brother Vitālijs to be conscripted into the Latvian SS Waffen.[4] And our family had known sympathies toward the Soviets.

When Augusts heard this, he brushed it off with characteristic disdain, saying, "If they do come, they will only take me." He reported the same to his wife, Helēna, hours later, assuring her that women and children would be safe if it ever came to an arrest.

Events would prove otherwise.

As the mounted horsemen traveled to Rusišku sādža, a few miles down the road from the Malta guardhouse, Augusts was handling cattle on his farm. A Polish neighbor saw the policemen with their wagons heading toward their hamlet of Rusiški, and he shouted, "Pan August! Police! They're coming! Dozens of them! They have wagons! Guns!"

A tall, well-built man of fifty-four, Augusts bounded out for his house and was nearly breathless when he rushed into his home. He was nearly gasping as he ordered his sons to go to the sauna and gather up the Soviets who were staying there.

His eyes narrowed in that way his sons recognized only too well. It was his authoritative, admonishing look he gave whenever he disciplined them. He commanded them, "Run as fast as you can toward the north, for the swamp at Lubāna!"

Augusts's wife, Helēna, dropped the knife she was using to cut cucumbers for the noonday meal and moved back her chair and quickly started collecting provisions for Augusts, his brothers, and the Soviets. She handed a bundle holding food for Augusts to take.

He brushed it aside. "I'm not leaving," he said as he directed his sons to move faster. His sons Broņislavs and Vitālijs spoke almost in unison and with great impatience, "Father, come, go!"

But he replied, to their utter disbelief, "They won't take me!" He waved them off. "Go! They won't take me."

But moments later, they did.

The Arrests

Police also seized Helēna and shoved her into the cart next to him. One policeman trained a gun on my grandparents as they looked on helplessly at the chaotic scene unfolding in front of them. It all went in so many directions with such blinding speed that it seemed as though the whole world was spinning around them.

MARIJA PLATACE FUTCHS FINE

Officers peeled off in the direction of two other Platacis houses. Some policemen rushed to the home of Augusts's brother Kazimirs. They seized him and shoved him onto the cart next to Augusts and Helēna.

Other police went to my father's home about one thousand five hundred feet away, down by the river in Malta. The soldiers saw my mother preparing lunch. They stormed in and barked out to her, "You're under arrest! Take your baby and come with us. Now!"

I was not yet ten months old. Solomeja picked me up from the wooden crib my father had built for me just one year earlier. It hung from a long birch pole that ran across the ceiling, allowing my mother to gently rock me back and forth. Now the crib snapped back and forth after my mother quickly grasped me up from it and wrapped a shawl around me.

That was the last time I would ever be in a crib. Before leaving our home, soldiers took three horses and killed a calf that they threw onto one of their carts. They loaded sacks of grain and flour they found in the barn and tossed them up onto one of the wagons. They set a torch to my father's home, a scene my mother could only watch in terrified horror.

While police were arresting adults in the three homes, other officers fanned out to hunt for my father and his brothers. Police saw the figures of my father and his fellow partisans dashing off through the forest toward the north. There were nearly one dozen of them, racing in desperately through snow-covered fields in the direction of the Lubāns swamp thirty-one miles northwest of our home.

With their loaded guns cocked, the police aimed at the half a dozen men in their sights. They were Broņislavs, his two brothers, and one Soviet, Ivan, who was taking up the rear. As Ivan frantically brushed away the footprints in the snow with birch branches, the Germans shot him dead on the spot.

Other soldiers continued to shoot at the fleeing partisans. But Broņislavs and his brother, Vītālijs, outran their pursuers. They made it to the swamp where they hid out for the duration of the Nazi occupation.

By this time, the Malta police battalion had my grandparents, great-uncle, mother, and me secured in their wagons. My family watched, powerless, as troops destroyed Augusts's animals, leaving one sickly horse behind. They left Augusts's house untouched.

The police saw Leonora and her older sister Malvīna sitting on top of the big furnace in their home. Leonora, then ten years old, started crying. She begged the soldiers to take her with her parents. The guards brushed past her and shouted, "Out of the way, toad! We're not taking you anywhere!"

Brother Jāzeps took cover. Even though he—at fourteen years of age—was ten years younger than his uncles, he had joined them in some of the raids they made on transportation lines that the Nazis used.

Captured

With all of us squeezed in the wagons among the food the soldiers looted, the Latvian Police Battalion lined up on either side of the wagons, forming a caravan. They set course for the town of Rēzekne, about sixteen miles to the north. As we moved past my father's house, it was engulfed in flames. The wooden home Broņislavs had completed building for my mother and me was gone.

Confused and dazed by the chaos and destruction, questions raced through the minds of my mother, Helēna, Kazimirs, and Augusts. My mother wondered if her husband escaped the police. She heard the shots and wondered if one of them brought down Broņislavs.

The once quiet life of the farming family into which she married and hoped to continue in as a new mother went up in a hot flash. Events were beginning to break down every defense she had.

All during that cold journey, Helēna could not stop wondering about those two contradictory comments Augusts made in the last twenty-four hours. The day before, he had assured her of her safety, saying, "They will only take me!" But just a few hours ago, when the police entered their door, he waved off everyone who told him to run, asserting with his characteristic confidence, "They won't take me!"

Was he saying that to calm her and them? Was it an involuntary statement spoken in a moment of panic, denying the obvious? It didn't matter. Nothing made any sense at this point.

Kazimirs Platacis, Augusts's brother, must have regretted allowing himself to be dragged into all this. He was not a partisan, although he was forced into giving support to one partisan activity due to his skills as a tailor.

His brother and nephews met Soviet paratroopers who landed on nearby August Hill. Some of them tore their parachutes. They entreated him to use his tailoring skills to mend them. At first he refused, but when they threatened to kill him, he relented. He worried about who would support his wife and children if he were caught.

Hadn't he taken special measures by burying those parachutes in the apple orchard next to his home? All those precautions were for naught.

As for Augusts, what thoughts must have raced through his mind? There were so many. Why was his family sitting next to him in the cart? Why didn't they just go after the ones who ran off?

Wasn't it true what he heard, that Germans would not take women and children? They saw but didn't take his daughters, Malvīna and Leonora.

Why were they taking Helēna? Why were they taking his daughter-in-law Solomeja and his granddaughter Marija? Were the Germans holding them hostage until they found Broņislavs and his other sons? Would they kill him if they couldn't capture his sons?

What, perhaps, he did not know was that even if the local police had caught my father and uncles, they still would have taken all of us: Kazimirs, Helēna, my mother, and me. The political reality then in 1944 was that Germans were losing, and certain readjustments in their war strategy were necessary as a result.

Where the Latvian battalion used to kill partisans off immediately in the early years of the war, they now needed them as forced laborers in German camps. That included family members, who, though they were not active partisans, became political prisoners merely for being related to partisans.

But the one burning question that kept coming back to Augusts on that ride from Andrupene to Rēzekne was, who tipped off the police? He knew the Platicises were under suspicion for months, but their arrest was based on someone's betrayal. Who could it have been?

Local people sympathetic to the legionnaires were monitoring their activities and reporting back to the local Latvian police. The Germans had already co-opted local Latvians in their espionage. It was a small community of only a few dozen persons, so my family could not keep its partisan activities secret for very long.

Within days of the arrests, one person and his family quietly left Rusišku sādža and never returned. The Platacis family would not know for weeks who betrayed them.

My family was about to be swept up into the terrifying stream of forced evacuations, incarcerations, separations, tortures, and murders. My once-large, close-knit, prosperous kulak family[5] was gone forever. One thing was certain: the coming months and years would be uncertain and terrifying.

All this commotion was lost on me as a ten-month-old infant. Having only the implicit memory of a baby, I could only register the emotional pangs of those few hours that would stay frozen in my system for the rest of my life.

Ever since I learned that my family and I were like tiny particles of sand swept up in the tidal wave of World War II history, I became obsessed with finding out what that time was like and how that experience impacted my mother and me. I began to learn about what psychologists call absent amnesia, which influences habits and other implicit learning without leaving any trace of that episodic memory.[6]

Augusts Platacis and Malvīna Platace, my grandparents

Helēna Platace,
Augusts's second wife,
my step-grandmother

Leonora Platace,
Helēna's daughter,
my father's sister, my half-aunt

Photos from Leonora Platace's family album

Broņislavs Platacis, my father

Vitālijs Platacis, my uncle

Alberts Platacis,
my great-uncle

Antons Platacis,
my great-uncle

Photos from Leonora Platace's family album

Kazimirs Platacis,
Augusts's brother, my great-uncle

Jāzeps Platacis, Helena's son,
my half-uncle

Augusts's house, ca. 1930

Photos from Leonora Platace's family album

CHAPTER 2

The Platacis Family

Pan August! Pan August!

Family Time

AS AUGUSTS WORRIED over the impending fate for his family members, a flood of memories came to him, images of happier family times.[1] The pictures flashed through his mind again as the police carried us over the snow-covered roads to Rēzekne. He had the foreboding sense that memories of times past would be all that would sustain him in the coming days.

As the five of us sat huddled together on the wagon, Augusts's thoughts went back to times when he and Helēna were raising their children on their successful farm. His fondest memories were those Sunday afternoons when the immediate family gathered, and other family members dropped in to catch up on the events of the past week. One Sunday stood out, the last one in September 1942.

In his mind Augusts saw eight of them traveling from Sunday service at the Andrupene Roman Catholic Church to his village of Rusiški. Their village had nine homes, five of them inhabited by the Platacis family. They rented out the remaining four to other farmer families.

Four adults were on horseback. Augusts and Helena led the procession, with Broņislavs and Solomeja, also astride a horse, following close behind. A gaggle of children—Jāzeps, Jānis, Malvīna, and Leonora—were running alongside this family column, with older brother Vitālijs joining them.

Helēna, a woman of ample size and gentle bearing, sat comfortably behind Augusts on their horse. She wrapped her arms around his waist, which was now a medium-sized paunch. Her embrace was something Augusts cherished as he had a passion for Helēna.

If he saw her talking to another man, he would sometimes ask her afterward, "Do you like that man?" They were born in the same year, 1890, in different parts of the Russian Empire. She was born in its Latgale region and he was born in St. Petersburg.

This was the second marriage for both the widower and widow. Augusts's first wife, Malvīna, had a sweet, attractive, and dignified presence. Before she turned thirty years, she died in childbirth while giving birth to her fourth child.

Malvīna bore Augusts four children. The first was my father. Vitālijs followed two years later in 1921. There were two more: Jānis, who came in 1926, and Andris, who died within months of her delivering him in 1927, following his mother's death.

Augusts's firstborn and his wife had been married for two years. Solomeja was also perched behind her man, holding onto him around the waist. She was one year younger than Broņislavs, small and slim, well matched with her husband in terms of their physical size. Broņislavs was the shortest of all the Platacis men, whereas his younger brother Vitālijs had the same tall build as his father.

As the horses trotted along the dirt road to Augusts's home, they went past the wheat and rye fields that they farmed during the week. Running ahead of the horses at times and scampering behind them at other times were the four children of Augusts and Helena.

Vitālijs loved racing against Jānis and stepbrother Jāzeps. Both boys were ten years younger than their older brother. Jānis and Jāzeps loved competing against their older brother. They looked up to Vitālijs, impressed by his daring actions as a partisan, a dangerous activity that Jāzeps had begged his father and older brothers to join.

The sisters, Malvīna and Leonora, struggled to keep up with their brothers, who had lean and fit physiques compared to their plump figures. Malvīna was eleven years old; Leonora, just eight. Every now and then Vitālijs reached down and gathered up some peas that were used to feed horses and threw them at his kid sisters. They caught them and threw the peas right back in his face.

Jāzeps grabbed some oats in hopes of lobbing them at Vitālijs, but the older brother always managed to outrun him. Jānis had his own mischief in store for all his siblings. He sneaked up from behind the girls and grabbed them around their waists, scaring the wits out of them.

Augusts looked with some pride at his landholdings that his father, Silvestrs, gave to him. He had the largest amount of property among his brothers. As his brothers knew all too well, Augusts was his father's favorite. He was the first to build a house, one so well constructed that it was, decades later, moved to nearby Malta, where it is home for another family today.

Silvestrs, who had served in the Russian Imperial Army for close to twenty years, was a stern taskmaster. He chided Augusts's brothers— Kazimirs, Antons, and Alberts—that they were still living in "dugouts." He admonished them, "You will all freeze there. Look at Augusts and follow his example."

Family Music Hour

Latvians are born into a singing nation, and the Platacis family exemplified that. Once they arrived home, the family music hour started. Although he was not musically inclined, Augusts encouraged his children to learn musical instruments and to enjoy singing.

Broņislavs and Vitālijs did both. They learned to play more than half a dozen instruments between them. Though music ran through their genes, as it does in most Latvians, the brothers excelled at it, especially my father. He played the accordion, balalaika, and mandolin and anything else he could lay his hands on. He was a natural entertainer. He and brother Vitālijs were the lead musicians in family settings and at community gatherings.

Helēna set the tone. As a devout Catholic, she gave readings from the Latgalian Bible and then gave a nod to Broņislavs and Vitālijs to sing a church hymn. Then they continued with the party songs. The two brothers took turns acting as master of ceremonies. My father was famous for throwing in a joke or two. He loved to imitate traveling salesmen and Gypsies.

After they sang the church hymn, Broņislavs made an announcement. "Solomeja and I are going to become parents, sometime in May next year."

Augusts smiled broadly and said, "A grandchild for my firstborn son! Congratulations, Broņislavs. Everyone, let's guess when my next grandchild will come. I say it will be May 19."

Everyone joined in giving his or her dates. Jānis said it would be May 22. Vitālijs said May 1. At the end, Rozālija said, "It's going to be May 30!"

Helēna said, "What good news this is in these Time of Troubles."

Vitālijs agreed, "Brother, sing that *daina*[2] when you were courting Solomeja."

Others chimed in, "Yes, Broņislavs, and play your balalaika when you do."

Music was, in fact, important to both the expectant parents. Broņislavs had met Solomeja in the church choir. That was when he asked her to go to his home to hear him perform for the family on Sundays after church, just as he did that day in September. He took out his balalaika and began to croon the "Heavenly Wedding:"[3]

Rode the Thunder and the Lightning
To the wedding of Sun's daughter
Riding over and away
Striking down the golden oak
She of sad days wept so dearly
Picking up the golden branches
And when they were all collected
She did spin a golden wreath
Placing it upon her head
She went off to the West
All the men were quite amazed
Where did you get such a crown?

As my father finished his song, the family began to break off into smaller groups. This was one of the times when Helēna and Augusts taught their children skills that would help them as adults, whether it was at home or in some kind of trade.

Apprenticeship

Formal education in the farming region of Andrupene went up to the fifth grade and included the basic subjects like science, math, and language. Children walked 1.8 miles each way to school. Broņislavs and his youngest sister, Leonora, completed all five grades. Math was his best subject, but memorizing poems was a problem. Leonora was an excellent student, receiving the top score—5—in every course. Her best subjects were nature and biology. Only math and algebra did not come as easily for her.

Because formal education in Latgale did not teach how to farmwork or develop skills for various trades, it fell to the parents to train children in an occupation that would earn them a livelihood. In that regard, Augusts and Helēna were nonpareil as teachers.

They instructed their sons and daughters in the outside "laboratory," the fields, where they walked them through the tasks essential for successful farming. The parents also ran the indoor one-room schoolhouse, where Helēna taught her daughters the domestic arts and Augusts taught his sons occupations related to commerce.

Augusts proved himself to be an excellent disciplinarian. Whenever the children started to misbehave during their lessons, he brought them in line without having to use any physical punishment. He had "this look" where he narrowed his eyes that settled into a penetrating gaze, and held that stare just long enough before the misbehaving child melted into submission.

Helēna's Girls

Solomeja, and Helēna's daughters, Malviīna and Leonora, headed for the kitchen to start preparing for the main meal, following Helēna's lead.

Augusts's children loved Helēna. She had that special quality, genius if you will, at merging three families into one harmonious household.

She won over the children from Augusts's marriage to Malvīna. She brought in Vladislavs, her son from her previous marriage. She brought in the three children she had with Augusts. She blended his family, her family, and their family into one harmonious unit.

In the small kitchen, the four of them—the two women and two girls—managed to move around without any friction. Normally, they had simple fare—potato, bread, milk, sour cream, and butter. But today was a special day. Broņislavs had an important announcement to make, and that called for some homemade dishes that would show off each person's culinary skills.

Solomeja took out the salted, dried meat and arranged it on a plate. She was not Helena's—or Augusts's—first choice for Broņislavs, something Solomeja knew all during her courtship with Broņislavs.

Solomeja came from a large family with Polish origins. Her name was the Latvian form of the Polish name Salomea, meaning "peace." There were eight members in her immediate family: six children with parents Ivan Danovskis and Valusja Danovska. The four daughters included her, Leonora, and Valentina. Unknown were the names for the fourth daughter and the two sons, all of whom died at early ages.

She did not have the sparkle and wit of her younger sister, Leonora, which may have made her feel somewhat intimidated by the large, talented, extroverted, and outwardly confident family members that Augusts headed. He had standing in the community. He was the patriarch of a family with deep roots in Rusiški.

The Danovskas were relatively recent arrivals. There were no surviving members of her mother's family who could hand down Danovskis family lore such as Leonora has done with the Platacis family.

But even if Solomeja was not Helena's first choice for a daughter-in-law, she appreciated how her daughter-in-law acquitted herself in the kitchen. Solomeja introduced Polish stuffed cabbage rolls and cucumbers in sour cream after she joined the family.

Leonora, the quick learner she was, fixed the chicken salad with a recipe her mother had taught her. She cut into pieces the chicken meat she had cooked in butter and milk, then added paprika, salt, and black pepper. She mixed in diced onions and poured the contents into a serving dish. "Taste it, Mommie," she said as she held up a spoonful to Helēna.

Helēna tasted it and said, "Good girl! You're already on your way to being an excellent cook."

Leonora would watch to see who took a second helping of her salad. The one person she knew would love it was her favorite brother, Jānis. Her one dish that he craved more than anything were her bacon pasties, the *pīrāgi*. She always made an extra one for him that she gave to him in secret.

Sister Malvīna cut the rye bread that Helēna had prepared the night before, a weekly activity that would feed the family through the next week. Helēna showed her daughters how to get the right proportion of dough to water, making sure the dough never turned solid. Helēna would leave it to Malvīna and Leonora to form bread loafs and bake them in their oven, which was really a furnace, ideal for baking bread.

Cooking was just one domestic skill that Helēna taught her daughters. She also instructed them in homemaking skills such as cleaning clothes and knitting. She taught Leonora how to knit the leggings that she was already making for the baby due in May 1943.

Helēna also found ways to have the siblings interact cooperatively with one another, often mixing gender roles. She had the little boys wash their sisters' feet. This ritual often followed the "earthy but pleasurable" experience that the children had when they shepherded animals during cold weather. To keep warm, they would stand for several minutes in hot cow dung to keep their feet warm.

Augusts's Boys

While Helena had her girls prepare the main meal of the day, the men were in a corner of the house where they had made a work area. Before the main Sunday meal, they reviewed the products that they had prepared the previous week.

Vladislavs joined the men who reviewed the quality of their output. Augusts taught his sons how to handcraft saddlery for horses, which included halters, leads, whips, crops, spurs, and reins. He also made winter clothing, wove baskets, and created macramé.

Augusts took the goods he and his sons had crafted the previous week and sold them at the market. When he returned with money from the sale of their goods, he would share the money fairly with all his sons.

He was an enlightened father who wanted his sons to develop a skill set that suited their interests and talents. He urged them to take whatever he taught them and then carry that talent as far as they could, even if it meant branching out in a new direction.

Augusts used leather and fabrics to create his products. Broņislavs's passion was working with wood. He loved going into the forest, taking timber from the trees, and creating saleable goods out of them.

On that one Sunday, Vitālijs remarked on how much they all admired their father's craftsmanship, farm acumen, horsemanship—the list went on. But then he looked at his father with a twinkle in his eye and said, "You know, Dad, you may know a lot about horses, but the one skill you lack is riding the metal horse!"

Vladislavs joined in, "Right! Remember that time we fixed the roof for that Briedis guy over in Malta, where we made enough pay to buy three bicycles?"

Augusts nodded, looking somewhat embarrassed at the same time. He knew what was coming next.

"So," Broņislavs said, "we rode the bicycles home and showed you our new form of transportation. And you thought there was no trick to it. You were the expert horseman. You even bragged, 'There's no trick to it at all. It'll be just like riding a horse, only a metal horse.' But then when you got on my bicycle, you went round and round in circles and crashed into the barn wall and wounded your head!"

Augusts laughed along with his sons. He was the kind of man who could take a joke on himself. "It's time to get to the table, sons," he said, as they made their way to the rectangular table that was in the area right next to the kitchen.

Family Meal

It was usual for the Platacis family to spend three hours at the Sunday family meal, because other relatives would come and go in the course of that time. While the children were present, the topics of conversation were all about family and farmwork.

Malvīna and Leonora were very close, separated in age by three years. They often enjoyed sparring with each other, using their Latgalian names for each other, Maļa and Ļoņa. Older sister Maļa decided to tease Ļoņa about what she did at the funeral events for Grandfather Silvestrs two years earlier.

Funeral observances started at home. Everyone—Father Augusts, Helēna, the children—were there. Maļa said Ļoņa looked into the open casket, where she saw her grandfather's ring on his finger and cross around his neck, both of which Ļoņa greatly admired.

Ļoņa glared at her older sister and said, "How dare you bring that up!"

But Maļa went right on with her story. She described how her younger sister continued to fix her gaze on the gleaming objects. She wanted to reach down and take them for herself, especially the ring. Imitating her sister as she looked to Father Augusts, she whispered, "Father, that's expensive jewelry. It's stupid to bury it."

"Stop it. Someone throw another potato at her nose," Ļoņa retorted.

This comment angered Malvīna, who recoiled at the very mention of that time when someone threw a potato that made a perfect landing on her nose. After that, she had a curved nose line.

"Ļoņa!" Malvīna shouted back. "You're the one who probably threw that potato at me!"

Malvīna shook her head. "No, I wasn't the one who did it!" and she continued the story. "So the family brought the casket to the cemetery and opened it again."

At this point, Vitālijs entered into the conversation, "Yes, I remember that. People had one last chance to say good-bye. The priest said the last prayers."

Augusts added, smiling at his daughter with affection, "Then my father's casket was closed, and they put him underground. But you, Leonora, still insisted that you wanted his ring. And what did I tell you?"

Leonora answered, "I'll never forget it. You said, 'No one will allow you to take it. Besides, what a dead man owns, he owns it for eternity.'" He then gave both girls a hug.

After the children finished eating, they went outside to play with the family dog, Duksis, while the adults talked on other subjects. No matter how it started—going over the crops, the weather, or the livestock—it always ended on politics, especially in these difficult times. They had experienced two occupying forces in as many years, first the Russians, now the Germans.

As one of the prominent kulaks in the village, Augusts had strong political views and wasn't afraid to express them. Rusiški villagers looked to him with respect, calling him Pan August. That way of addressing him involved dropping the *s* in his given name and using the title, *Pan,* Polish for sir.

Vitālijs brought up his admiration for Augusts's nationalist pride. He wanted to see a free Latvia. All three sons recognized that although their father was born in Saint Petersburg and served in the Russian Imperial Army, he was an avowed Latvian nationalist.

Vitālijs spoke up, "I remember, when Russians came the first time in 1939, our neighbor, that Russian lady Palageja, cried out, 'Pan August! Pan August! The Russians are coming!'"

"Yes!" Broņislavs broke in. "And you, Father, the great admirer of our first president, would curse in Russian, 'Screw the Russians. Ulmanis will still come!'"[4]

He knew he could curse when his sons were grown-up, as they were now. He never did in front of them when they were children.

Kazimirs and Rozālija

Moments later, when Augusts's sister Rozālija and brother Kazimirs came for their usual Sunday visit, the children returned to the table. They were eager to talk about the baby, who was arriving in May 1943.

Kazimirs's wife, Jādviga, brought a dish of cottage cheese for which she was famous in the village. Kazimirs was ten years younger than Augusts, born on January 14, 1900, in Andrupene.

Kazimirs owned a share of the property that his father meted out to each of his four sons. Silvestrs owned 15.61 hectares (38.57 acres) and meted out 2.610 hectares (6.4 acres) to Kazimirs. In addition to being a property owner, he was the manager of a tailor's workshop.[5]

He was a man of real dignity who did well with his tailoring business. He had also served with distinction in the military in the Latvian army and was a devoted family man. One photo of him showed him in uniform as a junior noncommissioned officer, *or jaunākais apakšvirsnieks.*

Nevertheless, Kazimirs had something of a checkered past, which he kept to himself. Not even his children or my aunt Leonora ever heard about his arrest for arson. It landed him in the newspapers three times. *Latvian Soldier* reported,[6]

> On the 25th of May, 1928 Kazimirs Platacis from Rusišķi village burned the living quarters, cowsheds and barn of Jekimovičs out of revenge. The arsonist was arrested.

Two newspaper articles followed up on that incident.[7] The first one was a plea from Kazimirs Jekimovičs and Jānis Romans to give them land as a priority case. Their houses had been burned, and they needed to rebuild urgently. The municipality responded that it accepted the case.

Though there were newspaper announcements about the arson incident, there was no mention why it even occurred. Kazimirs's children never heard about it; nor did Augusts's.

Rozālija's daughter, Helēna, squealed with delight when she heard Broņislavs and Solomeja were expecting a baby. Malvīna, Leonora, Jānis, and Jāzeps knew what was coming next. Young Helēna launched into the story about how she was a bringer, a member of the wedding party when Broņislavs and Solomeja married two years earlier.

Augusts's sister Rozālija pulled up a chair and dived into the chicken salad that Leonora had made as she listened to her daughter reminisce about the spring wedding in 1940. Young Helēna remembered Broņislavs arriving at Solomeja's home to show his intent that he wanted her to be his bride. She liked it that Broņislavs enlisted her as one of the bringers, because she loved to see how he had to "buy the bride."

"Do you remember, Broņislavs," she asked, looking at him, "that day Vitālijs, you, and I set out on horseback to Solomeja's home?" My father nodded as Helēna continued in the rapid manner of talking that she had. "You brought a dowry box from your family to Solomeja's house. It was tethered on top of that slow poke of a cow that Vitālijs has."

Vitālijs jumped into the conversation, "Don't talk about Gaida like that."

But his brother came right back at him, saying, "Well, her name fits, doesn't it? *Gaida* means 'to wait for.'"

Young Helēna interrupted Broņislavs. "Let me finish!" she said with some impatience. She talked on, describing how Solomeja was waiting in her house with other women. Finally, after Broņislavs and his bringers arrived, one woman emerged from the Danovskis home.

Helēna asked, looking in the direction of Vitālijs, "Do you recall the first woman out of Solomeja's home, her grandmother disguising herself in old clothes and covering her head? She looked hilarious."

Vitālijs responded, "Yes! I laughed so hard when I saw how she beckoned to you, Broņislavs, pretending she was your bride."

Broņislavs laughed and joined in, "Yes, I shouted my refusal to grandmother Danovska, 'You're not the one!' And of course, Solomeja's family members replied, 'If you want the real one, throw some money!'"

Vitālijs started laughing as well, and as he looked at Broņislavs, he said, "And then, right on cue, you threw out some lats,[8] coins, from the dowry box right at the entrance of the Danovskis home. I worked hard to get you the extra lats. You still owe me, brother."

Solomeja looked up after she took a sip of tea. "I wanted it to go on as long as possible, to see how many lats you were willing to throw in to win me."

Broņislavs broke in, "So that's why you made it go so long! After half a dozen women came out, I really had come down to the last lats. So I shouted, 'I'm almost out of lats! I need to give what's left to my bride. Where is she?' Then you appeared, and I shouted, 'She's the one!'"

Everyone talked about how the prenuptial event ended in an exchange of money from the groom's family in exchange for gifts from the bride's house. Everyone remembered it differently, what the Danovskis gave to the Platacis family and vice versa. People mentioned blankets, a scarf, socks, and gloves. All they agreed on was that Solomeja's family provided her a trousseau.

The conversation shifted immediately to the wedding. Rozālija remembered that Solomeja wore a white dress. Since it was early spring that day, April 9, 1940, she had taken dried flowers and myrtle and fashioned them into a wreath that held the veil on Solomeja's head.

Augusts's wife, Helēna, recalled that they all traveled three miles to the church on horseback. Rozālija enjoyed mentioning that her grandchildren served as the young attendants. The wedding party included the bringers, grandchildren, and choir members. The grandchildren and the choirboys scattered dried flowers at the altar, since flowers were not yet in bloom.

Vitālijs was the best man who brought the wedding rings. "Yes," he said, "Broņislavs and I made them by melting down two Latvian coins."

"That's all really nice," Leonora broke in, "but it was the wedding reception that was so much fun." She continued, "It took place at my father's home. Around twenty people were there. The tables were arranged in an L-shaped formation."

And then, with a giggle, older sister, Malvīna, added, "Father prepared a home-brewed ale that was very sweet, which you sipped, just enough to get tipsy but—"

Augusts, who was listening, ended Malvīna's sentence, "I warned you, Leonora, against getting proper drunk."

He added that by 3:00 a.m., everyone was exhausted and went home. The newlyweds slept in the main room on their wedding night, alongside everyone else. There might well have been ten people in that one room.

Wedding party members returned to Augusts's house around noon the next day for a late breakfast. There was still enough food left from the reception, so Helēna spread the remaining food out on the table, and everyone gathered around.

Vitālijs picked up from Malvīna to say he remembered that there was that other ritual for the newlyweds, one that would reveal who would be the boss in the marriage. "Remember the money challenge?"

"Of course," young Helēna replied. "I was there when the bride and groom arrived at Broņislavs's house. As the bringers threw money onto the floor, we watched to see who picked up the most money in the shortest time."

"And who won?" asked Broņislavs, looking at his bride, already knowing the answer.

"You, of course," Solomeja replied demurely.

The newlyweds, along with Broņislavs's family, spent the rest of the day at the Danovskis home. They ate, chatted, and socialized, returning back to Augusts's home in the evening.

More gifts followed. Augusts presented Broņislavs a cow and a horse. That inspired Broņislavs to make a winter sleigh out of wood that the horse would pull over the snow-covered ground in the nearby forest, the kind of ride he and his bride would enjoy.

The crowded quarters convinced Broņislavs to build his own home for his bride. Already skilled in carpentry, he and his brothers went out into the woods, chopped down trees, hauled them back, and built our home down by the river next to Malta, about one thousand and five hundred feet away from Augusts's home.

Augusts thought about those two years following the wedding, when his son spent his time farming alongside Solomeja and building their home. Broņislavs had around seven acres of land, four cows, and three horses, one of which was for transport. Solomeja milked a cow, made food for the family, and helped men with sowing and harvesting.

He recalled that his granddaughter was born on May 30, 1943, just as Rozālija guessed it would be at that Sunday meal in September. Augusts remembered that when Solomeja's water broke, Broņislavs took her to the sauna and told Vitālijs to go on horseback to get the midwife, a jolly old lady who lived a few miles down the road. She arrived shortly thereafter with Vitālijs. With the midwife assisting, my mother delivered the baby girl. My father gave her a jug of local brew that Augusts had made from grain, yeast, and bread.

Months before that, Broņislavs crafted his daughter's cradle as one of the last fixtures in the home he built. He constructed the crib for the baby out of birch wood and hung it from a long twelve-foot branch that was secured into the ceiling of the bedroom.

It was Leonora who came up with the name for the baby girl, Mārīte. She loved to play with ladybugs, for which the Latvian name is *bizbizmārīte or mārīte*, which is also a Latvian name. Just after his grandchild was born, she said, "She's small like a *mārīte.*"

Augusts was pleased that his son and daughter-in-law chose his niece, Monika, the daughter of his brother Kazimirs, to be the godmother; and he was doubly happy that they chose his son Vitālijs as godfather.

Now that they had a name for his latest grandchild, everyone in the Platacis family went to the church expecting to christen the baby girl Mārīte. But the priest said that a christened child had to have a holy name, a saint's name. Right there in the church, Broņislavs and Solomeja came up with a name that came closest to Mārīte. Her name would be Marija.

As Augusts lingered over these happy times, he knew that their arrest had destroyed the natural flow of courtships, marriages, and births of the Platacis family he headed. He was no longer Pan Augusts. He sensed that all his family members were trapped in an unstoppable horror, which someone—he didn't know who—brought upon them through an act of betrayal.

He feared for the youngest ones. Did his youngest son, Jāzeps, his fellow partisan, manage to escape? What about his daughters, whom the police left behind? Would they survive? And he couldn't erase that image of Leonora crying and begging the police to take her along with him and Helēna.

Andrupene Roman Catholic Church, 2014
Where my parents met and were married and I was christened

The kind of crib my father handcrafted for me
Andrupene Museum, 2014

Photos by Marija Platace Futchs Fine

CHAPTER 3

The Partisans

Time of Troubles

A S A CHILD of ten years, Leonora lived the turbulent history that she would tell me about seven decades later. What she knew then was that her father and uncles were mixed up in something exciting, so sensational, in fact, that they talked about it behind closed doors.

She knew to watch it all from a safe distance and not to walk into anything dangerous, but one day she almost did, when she brushed up against some legionnaires, pro-German partisans. She saw smoke in the nearby swamp while she was herding cows about one mile away from her home.

Being both brave and curious, she went exploring. She came upon the legionnaires, who glared at her and said, "Forget you ever saw us or we will drown you in the lake like a baby frog!"

She swore never to tell anyone, and didn't. The men who chased her away visited the herd owner for whom she worked on the same day. They cautioned him never to send animals in their direction again.

She knew her father, brother, and uncles were opposed to the legionnaires. In those years, Latvia was in the middle of a struggle between Germany and Russia. She heard her father saying several times, "Germans won't last!" Other times she heard the men say, "Hang on, the Soviets will come."

As partisans, the men in my family were involved in just one of several resistance movements that rose up against invading armies. Those forms of opposition have risen up several times in Latvia's history going back centuries.

Historical Antecedents

Neighboring countries—Poland, Sweden, Germany, and Russia—have occupied the small Baltic country. The Germans ruled Latvia (known then as Livonia), followed by Russia in the eighteenth century, which then subjugated it for three centuries.[1] For a brief period (1918-1940), Latvia was an independent country, only to be overrun by the Russians at the outbreak of WWII.

Thus, as of June 17, 1940, Latvia was boxed in between Russia and Germany. Both powers were warring against each other for domination of Eastern Europe, which included Latvia. The result was an overlapping series of invasions over a five-year period.

The Russians swept out the two decades of independence when they initiated *Baigais Gads*, Year of Terror (1940–1941), also known as Time of Troubles. The Soviets murdered or sent 35,000 to 40,000 Latvians to the gulags[2] in Siberia, events of that burned into the Latvian psyche a permanent fear and loathing for the Russians.[3]

Even in the eastern part of Latvia where Leonora lived, they heard echoes of the Year of Terror. It officially began on August 23, 1939, when Germany and Russia signed the Nazi Soviet Nonaggression Pact (also known as the Molotov–Ribbentrop Pact). Neither country upheld the two agreements, with the result that Germany and Russia divided the territories of Romania, Poland, Lithuania, Latvia, Estonia, and Finland into German and Soviet "spheres of influence."[4]

Within days, Germany invaded Poland on September 1, 1939. In the years that followed, one-third of the two million Latvians fled, were killed, or forcibly expelled. Some escapees jumped aboard shaky tiny boats headed for Sweden. Thousands died in the attempt to escape.

The German forces overtook the Russians in Latvia in 1941 and, at first, were welcomed as liberators. But Nazis proved to be an equally brutal occupying force from 1941 to 1945 until the Soviets regained control of Latvia in 1945, which would last five decades (1945–1991).

In this toxic climate, when occupying powers changed often and even overlapped for short periods of time in a particular region, no one could remain neutral. Siding with one side or another was a matter of survival. That was true for the Platacis men.

They felt squeezed between two longtime rivals, whom they viewed as identical evils. But they chose to side with the Russians for one reason: they believed Germany would lose. They wanted to provide themselves with some kind of insurance for the day when the Soviets would return.

The Platacis men also knew that the Hague Convention of 1907 made it illegal for Germans to conscript men in its occupied territory.[5] At the outset, Germans called it a voluntary conscription, which allowed Broņislavs and Vitālijs to refuse joining the Latvian SS Legion. Although Broņislavs was eligible due to his age (nineteen to twenty-three), he declined on the generally accepted grounds that he had a wife and was starting a family. Augusts's brothers Alberts and Antons were ineligible for service, since they were thirty-four and thirty-nine years old, respectively. While a few Latvians did voluntarily join the legion, their numbers did not satisfy the Germans, who started using more forceful methods on larger numbers of Latvians to enter the legion.

Viktors Rukmanis

Leonora said that sometime in the early 1940s Viktors Rukmanis, the local "governor" and Nazi collaborator, first entered as a menacing figure to our family. He came to public notice fourteen years earlier in a local newspaper. He placed a notice on September 5, 1930, that he had lost his Walther patent revolver and asked it to be delivered to the local police station if found.[6]

It was Rukmanis who went several times to my father's home to recruit him and my uncle into the Latvian Legion. Those rebuffs prompted him to confront my grandfather at Augusts's home, saying, "If you don't give us your sons, we will take you."

Augusts, the tall, commanding figure he was, looked Rukmanis in the eye and replied, "If that is the law, so be it," but he reminded him that it was illegal for Germans to force Latvian men into their combat units. Comments like that placed my grandfather and his sons under immediate suspicion.

While my father and uncle were able to avoid conscription into the Latvian Legion, one family member was not so fortunate. The son of Augusts's second wife, Vladislavs Geidāns, was forced into the SS Waffen when Nazis overran his village.

It's not clear what news the Platacis men heard, which led to their belief that Germany would ultimately lose. But there were signs that the Nazis were experiencing losses on many fronts. There were the Allied bombings of the Reich, the landings in North Africa and Sicily, the defection of Italy from the Axis camp, and the possibility of an early opening of an Allied second front in Europe.[7]

The two German defeats that my family surely must have known about were their staggering losses at Stalingrad and Kursk. Those setbacks emboldened partisans in all German-occupied territories; they were certain Soviet victory was inevitable.

An even greater setback for Germany was Operation Bagration,[8] a Soviet offensive timed exactly three years after Germany attacked the Soviet Union. That summer of 1944, the Red Army waged an all-out offensive, which, within just three weeks, left 350,000 German troops dead.

In late 1942 and early 1943, the Latvian Communist Party dropped Soviet leaflets from airplanes over Latgale. Messages included a call to arms:[9]

> Fight for Latvia's soil . . . the portentous moment has come when all the forces of the people must be pooled. Join the ranks of the active fighters against the German invaders, without distinction of rank or income.

Soviets needed to find people like my father, his brothers, and my grandfather to be part of the underground offensive against the German occupation, using guerrilla tactics to drive the Germans out.

Red Partisans

Latgale was an ideal place for finding that Soviet support. Red Partisans were already active in nearby Belarus and Ukraine.

Latgale—which was bordered by Russia and Belarus—was an obvious staging ground for Latvia. Latgale became one of the two centers of partisan activity in Latvia, and the other was in the swamps around Lubāns Lake. With the large Russian ethnic population in Latgale, Soviets had greater promise there to build resistance against Nazis than anywhere else in Latvia.

While it is true that my father and uncles felt no loyalty to Russia, the fact that the partisans were from Russia might have given my grandfather Augusts an additional motivation for siding with them. Both he and his father, Silvestrs, had served in the Russian Imperial Army before Latvian independence.

There is one undated picture from the Platacis family album that shows two generations of Platacis men: Silvestrs and his two sons, Augusts and Alberts. It was probably at the turn of the century when Silvestrs was in his early fifties and grandfather Augusts was in his late thirties.

That great-grandfather Silvestrs and grandfather Augusts were dressed in Russian military uniforms is interesting. Augusts was wearing a Marshals of the Soviet Military Russian Jacket, that later came to be known as the Stalin Jacket. It was belted and had a small strap parallel to the shoulder seam. Silvestrs was wearing a double-breasted Russian tank leather jacket.

It was possibly during the peak of formal partisan recruitment, in the latter half of 1942, that a classmate of my father, Oskars (whose last name is unknown), recruited Broņislavs to become a Soviet partisan. He, in turn, brought in brother Vitālijs and his teenage brother Jāzeps and their father, Augusts.

The Soviet resistance to Nazis took two forms, one led by Vilis Samsons (the Latvian Partisan Brigade) and one by Arturs Sproģis (the Red Partisans). Leonora did not know which group my grandfather, father, and uncle joined.

The evidence suggests they joined Sproģis's group. The time and place of their involvement and the activities they were engaged in point to their association with Sproģis. He began with small units, working his way from Russia to the Latgale region of Latvia.

MARIJA PLATACE FUTCHS FINE

That my father and grandfather housed Soviet paratroopers who landed at nearby August Hill also points to their possible alignment with Sproģis. The main thrust of my father's partisan activity—disrupting German transportation—was the kind of action that Sproģis's Red Partisans were known for. As one writer described it,[10]

> The summer of 1943 saw the beginning of the "war of the rails." From this time on, partisan attacks on the German-controlled railways were one of the main characteristics of partisan warfare; efforts to disrupt German traffic became the most important partisan military activity and remained so until the Germans retreated from the USSR. To a lesser extent the partisans also mined the highways, which the Germans used to supply their armies. All this activity required vast supplies of explosives and land mines.

Leonora said my father's participation in partisan activities lasted about six months, which would have begun around September 1943. That was about the time the operations of Sproģis were in full sway in the Latgale region.

That was when nine-year-old Leonora learned that brother Jāzeps was also in on this amazing family adventure. As his younger sisters would also learn, it wasn't just the Platacis men who were involved in this gripping action. Soviet paratroopers from Moscow also came into the thick of action.

Andrupene Partisan Headquarters

Augusts's home was a hub of all this clandestine activity. It was, in fact, the partisan HQ for Andrupene, where more than a dozen men went in and out to discuss how to assist Soviets in rearguard actions. That meant blowing up bridges and railroads that Nazis used for transport.

What was even more electrifying to the young Platacis girls was learning how their brother Jāzeps and uncles Broņislavs and Vitālijs went out to nearby August Hill in the dead of night to plant flares at the four corners on top of the hill to help guide the Russian pilot of the plane to the proper drop site.

Their parents allowed them to stand at the window where they could see August Hill in the distance. Planes from Russia sometimes made a quiet landing. That was when the Platacis men used walkie-talkies to coordinate communications as they offloaded armaments and other supplies to blow up railway bridges that Nazis used.

On the few occasions that Soviet paratroopers dropped down into the area, my father and his brothers brought them to the sauna in their home. There were seven Soviets living in the two Platacis homes.

Since Augusts knew Germans and their spies had been watching the Platacis men and their homes for months, he planned an escape route in the event of an arrest, whether it occurred in daytime or at night. To get a head start at night, he, his sons, and Soviets began to sleep outside their homes, ready to run at a moment's notice.

Surveillance

Augusts's nephew, Antons Galdiņš, was one of the last family members to warn him that Germans and their supporters, the legionnaires, were watching them. Other family members told Augusts the police had interrogated them. They were Antons and Alberts, my grandfather's brothers.

Neither one was a partisan, but local police questioned both about their father's rumored activity as well as whether his sons participated. Augusts thought that Nazi agent Viktors Rukmanis instigated both interrogations.

The news about the first interrogation came from Leonora. She reported to her father that several local policemen brought his brother, her uncle Antons, from Malta to Rusišku sādža to interrogate him in front of any Platacis family member who was at home. Leonora was the only one there at the time when members of the Latvian Police Battalion hauled Antons into her home and started questioning him. They asked which Platacis men were blowing up bridges and dismantling railway lines that the Nazis used.

Antons refused to give up his brother and nephews. At that point, the police took out two beams of wood, laid Antons on top of them, and started beating him with some kind of torture instrument. They tried to burn his toenails off with what looked like an industrial torch, but they couldn't get it to work.

Leonora cried and begged them to let her uncle go. She cried out, "He isn't guilty! He isn't even from Rusišku sādža."

They turned toward her and asked in a menacing tone, "How do you know?"

She stood her ground, saying, "He isn't from around here. He doesn't know anything."

He was black and blue from his ordeal, but they let him go and left.

Sometime later the police worked on Augusts's younger brother Alberts. They took him into the local Malta guardhouse for questioning. They had spared him the kind of punishment they meted out to Antons. Alberts reported to his older brother Augusts that he deflected all suspicions.

Impact of the Partisans

Despite all their efforts, the partisans had negligible success. The only two places in the Baltics where partisan activity reached any level of popular support or had any degree of success were in my father's area of Latgale and in Vilnius, Lithuania's capital. But even in Latgale, where there were more ethnic Russians than anywhere else in the country, the German sympathizers outnumbered the partisan supporters. That made partisan activity a highly risky enterprise for the men in my family.

The same could be said of the paratroopers; their efforts came to nearly nothing. The German forces or the local self-defense units eliminated almost all the Soviet partisan units who were dropped by air. They did not substantially weaken the German military, nor did they strengthen the Red Army.

Russians claimed to have many thousands of partisans, but by September 1944—half a year after the Nazi raid on my family homes—there were fewer than three thousand partisans operating in the Latgale area. By October 1944, the Red Partisan attacks ended.[11]

Some Soviet writers blame their meager results in Latvia on the lack of extensive forests, which could have more easily hid the movements of their guerrillas. But Russian and Belorussian districts, which had a comparable terrain, saw great partisan successes. Military historian John Armstrong argued that "the fundamental reason for the partisans' failure in Latvia was not the size or extent of forests, but the uniformly hostile human environment."[12]

Surviving in that setting would have required strong community support, which never materialized for the partisans. Russia's occupation left a scar on the Latvian population that was deep and lasting. Many Latvians, even in Latgale, had a dismissive view of partisans. Armstrong noted that,[13]

> the partisans were commonly looked upon by the population as desperadoes fighting for a lost cause, or as professional Communists having a stake in the regime.

Leonora underscored the lack of local community support for Soviet partisans. She said our family was shunned for their partisan involvement.

There are only rough estimates of the number of partisans whom Germans arrested and killed for being sympathizers to the Bolsheviks. Some figures go as high as eighteen thousand individuals. One newspaper article reported that SS general Haralds Puntulis, from 1941 to 1944, arrested a total of 967 Soviet partisans and their family members in Andrupene and surrounding regions. While the article doesn't name specific individuals, those arrests probably included my family of five.[14]

Puntulis, a native-born Latvian, was a platoon commander of the Auzsarg, which became the foundation of the Latvian quisling police. He commanded the fourth Rēzekne police precinct from 1941 to 1944, which included the Malta police station, the one closest to the Platacis farms. He not only targeted Jews and Gypsies but also sent more than five thousand non-Jews to Germany to be slave laborers.

For the year that my father and his brothers hid out in the unforgiving terrain of Lubāna swamp, they could draw on various kinds of support until Soviets took Rīga on October 13, 1944. They would have possibly joined other Soviet partisans who staged different kinds of resistance that did not threaten the German army and its military resources the way it did in Latgale.

Partisan efforts in Lubāna swamp area included terrorizing civilians, serving as lookouts for the Red Army, and creating lists of enemies of the Soviets that were later used for deportation and extermination of civilians. It is not known whether my father and his brothers participated in these partisan activities while they hid out in that region, but it is possible.[15]

My father and uncle could depend on rank-and-file peasants who would have helped them secure food, clothes, or information, since the Platacis men were not foreigners who had come from Russian soil. Instead, they were "one of them," speaking the same language and sharing the same background.

As the brothers Broņislavs and Vitālijs hid out in the swamps, their younger sisters and brother scrambled to adjust to the loss of their parents. On that day that the Latvian police came to arrest members of our family, Leonora and Malvina waited until they heard the last sounds of the departing horse wagons. They searched for Jāzeps, who fled to parts unknown and hid out for three days. His sisters had no idea if he had been caught up in the dragnet or was shot.

When he showed up unharmed, the sisters were relieved. They felt they could face the trials that were certain to follow as there were now three of them. They already had one immediate task at hand. Jāzeps helped them drag in a sick horse that soldiers had left behind. Try as they did to bring it back to health, nothing worked. They had to put him down.

The young man of the house prided himself for filling one sack of flour mixed with cow dung so that soldiers would see it and not take it. But being a resourceful lad, Jāzeps took care to secret away a clean sack of flour in a place where the arresting officers couldn't possibly find it and buried it three feet under the ground in their yard, covered by their tractor.

As the shock of the arrests wore off, Leonora realized that the three of them were now alone. But she thought that surely her parents, Uncle Kazimirs, Solomeja, and baby Marija would return. After all, the police didn't take her or Malvīna or the wife of Kazimirs, Jadviga. Maybe they would question her father and uncle and release them, just as they released her uncles Antons and Alberts after interrogating them.

The question still lingered for everyone in the family. Who gave up their family? In a small hamlet like Rusiški, secrets always find their way to the surface. While Jāzeps was in hiding for those three days, he talked with various villagers who watched the comings and goings of everyone. He found out who the traitor was.

August Hill, the parachute drop site now, 2014

Mākoņkalns, 2014

Photos by Marija Platace Futchs Fine

CHAPTER 4

Rēzekne Prison

I'm Sorry, Brother

Rēzekne

THE POLICE BATTALION took my family to Rēzekne Prison. While soldiers locked up Helēna, Solomeja, and me in one room, the Nazis put Augusts and his brother Kazimirs in another holding cell. It didn't matter to the men in command that Kazimirs was not a partisan; it was enough that he was related to one and had aided Soviets in mending some of their parachutes and acted as a messenger.

The town of Rēzekne was the second largest in Latgale. By the time the five of us arrived there on March 13, air bombing had wiped out two-thirds of the town's buildings. Around 6,500 of its prewar residents left or were killed, leaving just five thousand people behind in the city at war's end in 1945.[1]

During the German occupation (1941–1944), Rēzekne was under the control of Heinrich Lohse, the appointed Reichskommissar. Just as the Nazis appointed a Latvian, Haralds Puntulis,[2] to his station in Malta, they also lined up Latvian-born Boļeslavs Maikovskis,[3] as chief of II Section of the Rēzekne District Police. He would become a willing collaborator, occupying his position until the German retreat in late July 1944. Puntulis and Maikovskis possibly had a role in the arrest of my family.

Germany's political mission in Latgale was to destroy the Jewish population, settle ethnic Germans, rid the area of Soviet partisans, expel some of the native population, and Germanize the rest. Maikovskis acted at the behest of the Nazis all the way up to the close of the prison in July 1944, which meant he was there at the same time my family were imprisoned there.

It is likely that Maikovskis was the official who set in motion the surveillance, the interrogations, and the arrest of my family on March 13, 1944. He was possibly working through Haralds Puntulis and his agent, Viktors Rukmanis. When efforts at conscripting my father and uncle didn't work, Maikovskis possibly had Rukmanis lean on my grandfather Augusts, who defied the illegal conscription.

Rēzekne's prison was infamous during the Nazi occupation, as it was a staging ground for brutal tortures and murders. For that reason, it is incongruous that the jail stood directly across from the Rēzekne Roman Catholic Church of the Holiest Jesus Heart, one of the largest and most beautiful churches in Latvia.

During Germany's occupation from 1941 to 1944, more than eighteen thousand Jews, Gypsies/Roma, Soviet partisans, Russians, Latvians, and other nationalities died at the hands of Nazi soldiers and their collaborators at Ančupāni Hills. That is how it became known as the Killing Fields.[4]

Reprisals

The chief example of Nazi retribution against Soviet partisans was the whole-scale annihilation of Audriņi, a village located four miles north of Rēzekne. It stands out as the largest indiscriminate slaughter of any group of persons in Latvia. The Germans, with the help of their local Latvian police headed by Boleslavs Maikoviskis, eradicated the entire village. It served as a brutal reprisal for partisan activity and as a warning to other villages against harboring Soviet partisans.

Audriņi was a Russian town whose citizens observed the Orthodox faith, known as the Old Believers. There were forty-eight families, for a total of 215 inhabitants, including fifty-one children. The Audriņi citizens were inclined toward communism, which led Nazis to suspect their families kept Soviet partisans in their homes.

Police found one village woman, Anisya Glushneva, was concealing her son, a Red Army soldier, and five of his comrades. When the soldiers put up resistance, killing two Latvian soldiers, German security police commanded Maikovskis to "wipe the village of Audriņi off the face of the earth."[5] He "energetically responded," with Haralds Puntulis providing his enthusiastic assistance.

After looting food, clothing, and animals in the village, the Germans burned all forty-two farmhouses. Officers and local policemen then held a feast with food they plundered.

On January 3, 1942, Germans and Maikovskis's men took one hundred seventy Audriņi inhabitants to the nearby Ančupāni Hills and used pistols to kill them off. The police walked around piles of victims to finish off those who were still showing signs of life. They pushed all the children into the mass pits and buried them alive.

The next day, Maikovskis ordered his men to gather up townspeople and take them to the public square to watch the remaining thirty Audriņi citizens—mostly men and adolescents—file in. Police shot each of them.[6]

The Audriņi massacre served both as a brutal reprisal for partisan activity and as a warning to other villages against harboring Soviet partisans. The fact that Nazis used this as a warning to other partisans made me wonder if the news about that village reached the men in my family in Andrupene. How could Augusts and the others not know about it? My family's home was just sixteen miles from Rēzekne just a few miles outside of Audriņi.

The Platacis men heard enough about the German losses in far-off places like Stalingrad and Kursk, which gave them the impetus to join the partisans in the first place. So wouldn't they have known about German reprisals against civilians—men, women, and children—in their own region?

And if the Platacis men knew about the murders of men, women, and children in Audriņi, wouldn't Augusts have feared for his own family? The Nazis obliterated an entire town based on just the suspected ties its community had to Soviet partisans. Wouldn't my grandfather, father, and uncles—who were actively engaged in disrupting transportation lines the Nazis were using—have feared for their own families?

Audriņi was not the only case in point. Nazis had a history of taking swift retribution against anyone who resisted them, Audriņi being the most outrageous, far-reaching example of wholesale slaughter. When it came to conscripting Latvians into their legion—and they didn't get the number of volunteers they needed—Nazis took brutal methods, especially when it came to partisans. They killed the men and sent members of their families to concentration camps, sometimes doing both.[7]

The Audriņi massacre occurred eighteen months before Nazis imprisoned my family. Our arrest came within months of the Nazi occupation ending in Rēzekne in 1944. The lead-up to our arrests took a longer time than it did in the case of the Audriņi incident.

Yet, oddly, those acts of retribution, which others experienced in Latgale, never took place in my family for months on end. For some reason, Nazis passed up several occasions to arrest Augusts and his fellow partisans. Because they didn't arrest my family, did Augusts think he beat the odds? Did he assume the importance he had in the community shielded not only him but his family as well? I will never know.

When the arrest did happen, it resulted because of someone's betrayal. Until then, Augusts and Broņislavs probably thought there was no danger to their families. Whether they knew about the Audriņi tragedy or what happened to other partisans, they thought their women and children were safe.

While the Nazi's reprisal against the Platacis family was selective and not wholesale, they meted out brutality quite effectively. They arrested some but left behind some women and children to fend for themselves. That included the children of both Kazimirs and Augusts and Jadviga, the wife of Kazimirs.

Betrayal

We settled into the monotonous and dreaded existence of Rēzekne prison. In the first few weeks, prison officials allowed Kazimirs's wife to bring in food for him. Helēna and Solomeja worked in the kitchen. I remained with my mother.

On Easter, April 9, the family experienced the first aftershock following the March 13 earthquake that destroyed our home in Rusiški hamlet. Leonora's brother Jāzeps brought homemade butter and sausage for everyone at the prison.

For the first time, prison officials refused the food anyone brought. That was when the guards told Jāzeps that they shot Augusts, his father.

He would learn after the war from Kazimirs that the police tortured both his father and uncle but saved Kazimirs to perform a monstrous task against his brother in nearby Ančupāni Hills, three miles outside Rēzekne.

Because police beat Augusts so savagely, he was too weak to dig his own grave. They ordered Kazimirs to do that. After the younger brother did so, he went to the older brother, kissed him on the cheek, and said, "I'm sorry, brother." A soldier hit Kazimirs with his rifle for talking to Augusts, and then shot Augusts, who fell into the pit his brother dug for him. Digging his brother's grave had to have been a singular torment for Kazimirs. The frozen ground made shoveling a hole an agony all its own.

Germans were known for expending the least amount of time and effort for their murders. Having Kazimirs dig his brother's grave was one way of sparing soldiers the burden of doing it themselves. Germans also expected Kazimirs would tell others what happened to anyone who was a partisan, thereby getting the warning out through the person they forced to dig his brother's grave.

One other measure Germans took to save their energy was to order a prisoner to walk a certain number of steps from his grave before shooting him. That way, the murdered victim would fall into his grave without soldiers having to push or drag the body into the pit.

If that person was still breathing, soldiers chose not to shoot him in order to save their ammunition. That might have happened to Augusts. As he fell into the pit, he might have still been breathing.

Hearing about his father's death made the news Jāzeps had come to tell the imprisoned family even more heartbreaking. He revealed the identity of the person who betrayed the family.

It was Alberts, Augusts's younger brother.

When police took him into the Malta police station to question him about his brother's activities, Alberts told the Gestapo that Augusts and his three sons were the ones blowing up bridges, derailing railway tracks, and housing Soviet paratroopers. That's why they never tortured him. Now they had all the evidence they needed to arrest Augusts, his sons, wife, and family.

Alberts and his family were the ones that left quietly a few days after the arrest. No one ever heard from them again. The family might have guessed that Augusts's younger brother was the traitor. Alberts never had any signs of being tortured, whereas Antons had unmistakable signs of being beaten. Alberts must have caved in quickly; he came out of the interrogation without a scratch. He gave no report about being beaten.

Alberts represented just one—the most personal—kind of betrayal that my family was to know in the war. Local police, whose civic job was to protect them, betrayed them as well. They were the arresting officers working at the behest of the Nazis. It went even higher, to the Latvian officials such as Rukmanis, Maikovskis, and Puntulis, who collaborated, in each case quite willingly, with the Germans.

Leonora refers to the year that followed as the time "when the adults were taken away." That first winter was when she, Malvīna, and Jāzeps were on their own. The legionnaires prohibited them from going to school or traveling far from home. They lived on the flour Jāzeps had hidden, and some chickens. They put the milk in the river to keep it cool.

One of their uncles had sold the rye field next to their home to a local shopkeeper. The proceeds from that sale gave them enough money to survive in that year that Helēna was gone. The life of the wealthy kulak family Leonora had grown accustomed to disappeared. The food she ate was less palatable than what her wealthier friends enjoyed.

Imprisonment

The Rēzekne police kept Kazimirs, Helēna, Solomeja, and me prisoners for three months. I wondered why they held us there as long as they did. Might they have been holding us in the hopes they could capture my father and his fellow partisans, and then release us once they captured the escapees? But if that were the case, why did they capture Helēna when they had Augusts?

Whatever their reason was before June, there was no mystery why they moved us out that particular month. They had to evacuate everyone, since Russian troops were circling the city. They destroyed the meticulous records they kept on all their prisoners before they evacuated. Without any prisoner records, it fell to Aunt Leonora and Kazimirs to give the account of what happened during and immediately after in Rusiški and Rēzekne.

Of the nine Platacis family members involved in the Nazi arrest, three escaped and six were taken into police custody. Two of them were tortured, and Augusts, the paterfamilias, was murdered and buried at Ančupāni Hills.

Moral Dilemma

Wars always present a moral dilemma for people caught up in them, whether they serve in the military or are civilians. Kazimirs, Helēna, and Solomeja were about to face tests of their moral character. The dehumanizing conditions the three of them already experienced made the moral choices they had to make in order to survive all the more difficult.

The grief that Helēna and Kazimirs experienced after Augusts's torture and murder had to have a deadening effect on them. They both feared for their children.

Helēna knew no adults were around for her son and daughters. What, also, was the fate of her son from her first marriage, Vladislavs? Would he ever survive his forced conscription by the Nazis?

Great-uncle Kazimirs must have felt the terrible burden of seeing his brother tortured, shot, and then fall into the pit he was forced to dig for him. He must have wondered how his wife would manage without him. That was the reason he decided to help the Soviets repair their parachutes months earlier. They said they would kill him if he didn't repair them, so he did. What he tried to avoid by helping the Soviets was to no avail. Germans ended up capturing him. Now his family had no wage earner.

As for my mother, I think she could not take it all in. The flashbacks she had were discordant sounds of bullets firing off every second, bellowing animals, and my wailing as soldiers shoved us into the cart. There were the alarming images: flames licking up our home, soldiers looting food and valuables.

Although she is my flesh and blood and she passed her genes on to me that left me with certain predispositions, I have so little information to understand her. I have no picture of her. There is no member of her family who can tell me what her passions, interests, strengths, and weaknesses were. I only know some milestones in her life and some impressions of her from persons who knew her from a distance.

An image of her begins to form in my mind as she entered the prison. She knew her husband had eluded the Gestapo. That meant he might still be alive, unless one of those shots she heard brought him down. It was becoming harder for her to believe what he told her all during his partisan activity, that Germans would not take women and children. If that was so, why was she the prisoner with her infant?

She was the one person for whom the war would have the deepest, most negative, and long-lasting effects. She was one of the individuals for whom there would be no moral compass to guide her out of the madness of war. Historian Tara Zahra described the "discovery" of familial separation as the quintessential wartime tragedy for persons such as Helēna and Kazimirs, and especially Solomeja. It was[8]

> a major legacy of the Second World War. In the years
> that followed the war, the conviction that the separation
> of parents and children represents an irreparable form of
> psychological upheaval attained the aura of self-evident
> truth.

I think that is when my mother started to blame Broņislavs for what she was going through, a feeling she would carry to the end. As the days in the prison turned into weeks, she heard screams of tortured prisoners. Then she learned about Augusts's death and the betrayal of a family member, Alberts.

Once she learned all four of us were headed for another prison in Salaspils, a German concentration camp, I think she began to worry less for my father's well-being and more about how unfair it was that she was being held as hostage for him.

Helēna, Kazimirs, and Solomeja knew about the thousands of Latvians whom Soviets sent on trains to Siberia in 1941. Up until that day in June 1944, they felt fortunate for having escaped that dreaded journey. They would soon learn the Germans had their own version of the gulags. They were called concentration camps.

The soldiers took us to the next holding center, Salaspils "Death" Camp, on June 13, 1944. Leonora had no way of knowing that the worst lay ahead for her mother, uncle, Aunt Solomeja, and her baby, the one she had named Mārīte.

Rēzekne Prison (*foreground*), 2014
Roman Catholic Church of the Holiest Jesus Heart (*background*)

Photo by Marija Platace Futchs Fine

CHAPTER 5

Salaspils

Stolen Children

The Camp

LATVIAN OFFICERS TOOK my family and me, now thirteen months old, to Salaspils concentration camp.[1] Because towns in Latgale were under constant attack by Russian troops, soldiers might have taken us on an indirect route by truck from Rēzekne down to Daugavpils and then on a train 136 miles to the key military town of Salaspils.

The concentration camp was located outside the small town of Salaspils, twelve miles south of Rīga. Twelve thousand prisoners went through the camp during its existence from 1941 to 1944, including politically suspect Latvians such as the three Platacis adults, Kazimirs, Helēna, and Solomeja.

The camp's head officer, Konrāds Kalējs,[2] was a Latvian soldier who switched his political loyalties two times in three years. He served as a collaborationist for the Russians during their occupation of Latvia and then as a collaborator for the Germans under their occupation. In 1935 Kalējs joined the Latvian army as a cadet, becoming a lieutenant four years later. When Russia took Latvia in 1940, he joined the Red Army, which he deserted in 1941 to become a Nazi collaborator when the Germans captured Latvia as part of Operation Barbarossa.

As a member of the Nazi-controlled Latvian security police, he helped collect, interrogate, and transport "undesirables," including Soviet partisans who were political prisoners. As a company commander and first lieutenant of the Latvian Auxiliary Security Police (AKA

"Arajs Kommando"), he commanded one hundred men who murdered more than twenty-eight thousand people, ninety percent of them Jews.

Separation

Salaspils was the turning point of my life and for my mother. The Nazis carried out their procedure for any political prisoner who came with a child. They seized it from its mother.

Helēna saw it happen to me and Solomeja, who screamed and fought back against the guards. As I heard her cries of anguish, I must have wailed and reached out for her. I no longer felt the warmth of her body, but instead the cold, rough texture of the officer's heavy coat.

This forcible removal of mother from her child happened thousands of times in all the countries that Germany occupied. Germans kidnapped thousands of us as part of a secret program already entering into its ninth year. There was a witness in Poland who saw a seizure that was possibly not too different from what took place between my mother, the guard, and me:[3]

> I saw children being taken from their mothers, some were torn from the breast. It was a terrible sight: the agony of the mothers and fathers, the beating by the Germans, and the crying of the children.

Following the separation from my mother, the camp officers hung a tag around my neck with my name and date of birth on it.[4] They took me to one of the camp's two nurseries. The experience would have long-lasting effects of varying degrees on both of us.

Helēna found my mother inconsolable that first night. She cried until morning, unable get up for the work assignment. Her stamina was gone; she showed no strength to cope with what lay ahead.

Part of her angst was that she probably had no knowledge about the reasons behind our separation. Did the guard say he was going to kill me because I was the child of a partisan? Did he tell her that she was going to the concentration camps as hostage for my father? Or did he say nothing, leaving her to imagine the worst?

Solomeja's Angst

Multiple losses by refugees in general—and political prisoners in particular (such as my mother)—often led to feelings of overwhelming grief. The emotional reactions among refugee mothers who lost a child are similar to those associated with death. But they are more agonizing in wartime, when those feelings are mingled with frightening memories. Christ and others reported that[5]

> the few studies that have compared responses to different kinds of losses have found that the loss of a child is followed by a more intense grief than the death of a spouse or parent.

It's possible my mother was overwhelmed with a sense of purposelessness about the future, numbness, detachment, absence of emotional responsiveness, a feeling that life is empty or meaningless, a sense that part of herself died, and a shattered world view. After the liberation of Bergen-Belsen camp in 1945, case workers who worked with female inmates who had lost their children observed,[6]

> A grieving mother could express intense rage directed at the husband, at another family member, at God, at fate, or even the dead child.

I don't know what coping mechanisms my mother had, whether she had religious beliefs or the instincts of a survivor that could have lifted her out of her privation. It's not possible to know if my mother had any support from other women such as what developed among female inmates in places such as Bergen-Belsen concentration camp. Women there who lost children formed groups of friends who could allow a woman to grieve, to talk about what happened, ask questions, be patient, and find ways to memorialize a lost child.

She never reached out to Helēna, who could only watch Solomeja's actions in pained silence. They might have been assigned to different barracks, as Helēna never mentioned having any interactions with my mother. She mentioned no conversations she had with Solomeja in the camp, only sightings of her. That's when she saw Solomeja "taking up with a guard" and suspected she was pregnant at the time the three of them were taken from Salaspils to Rīga Harbor.

Infant Traumas

As I have tried to take in that experience of being separated from my mother, I began to read about infant traumas. Since they occur in infancy, before the hippocampus can develop explicit memory, those climactic events become part of infant amnesia. A cataclysmic event during that early period of infancy is stored in implicit memory, where "emotions and body sensations" become permanent.

While I obviously do not recall the event of being separated from my mother, Robyn Gobbel[7] explains that my body permanently stored the fear, the terror, the loneliness that I experienced at that time. It would take some equivalent experience to bring back the same feelings experienced earlier. At that moment, I would recall that feeling, if not the actual event itself. She called such an experience a participatory memory.

I think I experienced that kind of memory in 1996. I went through an explosive series of unexpected emotions at the time my husband, Irwin, disappeared for six hours. He had early-onset Alzheimer's disease, which changed the role I had from wife to parent.

Rather than assess the situation and act with calm deliberation, I was convulsed with tears and a terrifying sense of panic. All I could do was ask myself whether I should fight, flee, or freeze. Knowing decades later that a guard seized me from my mother, I think the feelings of loss, terror, and pain of that separation resurfaced at that time.

That same overwhelming sense of loss came back to me just months after I received files on my mother's incarceration in German camps. I cried nonstop for hours, long into the night. I had to call out to a friend to talk me through it.

Those intense emotional experiences are examples of the implicit memories that resurface when the body's stored memories of earlier traumas resurface, triggered by events that bring back the emotions of that event. Not all implicit memories such as mine lead to crying spells. There are the traumas in early childhood that lead to a lifetime fear of flying in airplanes, being enclosed in a small space, a fear of heights, etc.

I began to think a little differently about an involuntary hand position that I have awakened with every morning for as long as I can recall. My left hand is balled up in a tight grip. Initially, I thought it was an instinctive action that might have been triggered by an event in the Hahnenklee orphanage. Maybe I fended off an attack from some child in the night with my left hand because of the way that child awakened me in a threatening manner.

There was never any unpleasant sensation in waking up with my curled-up fist. I shrugged it off as one of those "unknowables" about my childhood. But after Leonora told me about the separation from my mother at Salaspils, I began to wonder: Did I punch at the guard with my left hand as he seized me? Did I clutch onto my mother with my left hand since the guard slammed me against the left side of his body?

But why did I use the left hand, when I am right-handed? I began to get a possible explanation when I examined a depiction of that brutal separation of a mother from her child at the Salaspils Memorial in 2014. Something about the child in the picture struck me. It was grasping onto its mother with its left hand.

That made me wonder. As the guard seized me from my mother, might she have been holding me on her left side? That would mean I had my right arm tucked inside alongside her body. My left arm was free, which I used, perhaps, to punch the guard and then used the same hand to grasp onto my mother. Whether it has anything to do with that separation, I now actually feel a pleasant sensation when I see my curled fist, because I feel I am touching my mother.

MARIJA PLATACE FUTCHS FINE

Lebensborn

It's doubtful whether guards told Solomeja what my fate would be, but seizing me was part of Germany's program for widening its circle of young Aryan recruits. In 1935 Nazis established Lebensborn ("Fount of Life"), which ended ten years later when the Third Reich collapsed.

The secret association had two components.[8] The larger one was kidnapping children with blond hair and blue eyes for adoption by a German family. Among these children were those such as myself, whom Germans branded as children of dissidents, resistance, or enemies of the state. As for the fathers of these "racially appropriate" children, they were shot or sent to concentration camps, leaving the children available for adoption. Since Nazis could not capture my father, my mother went in his place.

The Stolen Children program came under the leadership of the SS, the Schutzstaffel. On July 25, 1943, Heinrich Himmler,[9] the Reich leader (*Reichsführer*) of the SS of the Nazi party, ran the concentration camps and took command of orphans. Himmler was the first to give the order to seize all children who were racially acceptable, starting in Slovenia.

By the time I arrived at Salaspils, Lebensborn was already in effect in Poland, Luxembourg, Holland, Russia, Ukraine, Czechoslovakia, Romania, Slovenia, Yugoslavia, Estonia, and my native country of Latvia.

The numbers of children Nazis stole from dissidents were a fraction of the children they seized from Polish parents. Poland had a sizable German population, which provided the richest target for the Nazi's kidnapping program between 1940 and 1945. Some Polish estimates claimed Germans kidnapped two hundred thousand Polish children living in the German-occupied territory, but it is more likely the figure was closer to twenty thousand.[10]

Kidnapped children were either set up for immediate adoption by German couples or sent to orphanages until they could be adopted at a later time. Local staff ran these orphanages in the countries Germany occupied, such as the Latvians did at Rīga Orphanage. But they followed the dictates of Germans.

When German soldiers took kidnapped children to orphanages in their occupied territories, they sometimes changed the names of the children or erased the names of their parents. In my case, they did the latter, informing the orphanage staff I was illegitimate. This lack of documentation would present insurmountable problems for international agencies after the war when they tried to return thousands of kidnapped children to their biological parents.

After two months in Salaspils, Germans forced a camp evacuation, as they had done in Rēzekne, and for the same reason. Soviet troops were days from taking the camp. Before Germans emptied Salaspils on August 15, 1944, they took my mother, Kazimirs, and Helēna to Rīga Harbor. Soldiers boarded them on a boat for Germany to their respective concentration camps.

In those frantic weeks, hundreds of thousands of Latvians fled Rīga on any kind of transport available. Rīga Harbor was one place where thousands of people converged. After German supply ships unloaded their cargo at the ports of Rīga, Ventspils, and Liepāja, they took on refugees. Helena, Solomeja, and Kazimirs were among the Latvians boarding ships out of the harbor, except they were under armed guard.[11]

Many passengers on the ship came down with typhoid. It is not known if my mother was a victim, but my grandmother and great-uncle came down with it. They possibly contracted the disease in Salaspils camp. It can take effect anywhere from six to thirty days after exposure in confined, unclean places with high concentration of people, such as the camp they were in. That is why the scourge is often called the jail disease.

Typhoid, the plague of every war since the beginning of time, is known for bringing on a high fever over several days. If it is untreated, an infected person feels weakness for weeks, even months. Patients can also suffer from stomach pains, constipation, and a skin rash with rose-colored spots. The more acute cases include confusion, diarrhea, and vomiting.[12]

Helēna was so ravaged by typhoid that she crawled under a bench on the boat until the ship reached its destination, an action that probably saved her. Kazimirs told her to remain there to avoid detection. The two of them witnessed the horrifying sight of soldiers throwing the dead overboard. Helēna stayed hidden until someone on shore noticed her after the boat docked. Concentration camp officials took her along with Kazimirs to quarantine.

As they evacuated Salaspils camp, Germans followed their time-honored practice of destroying records and leaving behind anyone too weak to make it on their own. Soviets reported they found 632 corpses of men, women, and children dumped in the pond. The children who drowned had suffered from typhoid fever and measles, among other diseases.[13]

Germans took eight of us who were deemed healthy enough from the nursery and kept us in some undisclosed place in the area until September 2, when they took us to Rīga Orphanage. Guards presented me to the clerk at the front desk at the orphanage. The name tag wrapped around my neck gave my name, date, and place of birth. I began my life as an institutionalized child for the next four years.

Salaspils Memorial, 2014

Wall exhibit: Guards seizing children from their
mothers; child reaching to its mother's arm

Left to right: The Unbroken, Mother, Solidarity, Humiliation
Photos by Marija Platace Futchs Fine

CHAPTER 6

Concentration Camps

Taken Hostage for the Husband

SOLOMEJA, HELĒNA, AND Kazimirs were among the millions of people whom Nazis imprisoned in over fifteen thousand camps in fifteen countries.[1] The three of them arrived in Germany eight months before the Third Reich ended, a time Germany had stepped up its program of using prisoners from its occupied territories to keep its war machinery going.

To ensure that prisoners could work in the overcrowded, subhuman conditions of its camps, Germany set up quarantine units and recovery programs (*Erholungslager*) at selected locations. Stutthof was one of those camps, which confined all incoming prisoners who had typhoid or were carriers of the disease. It had experienced three typhoid epidemics in the two previous years. The most serious outbreak came at the end of the summer in 1944, just when my great-uncle and grandmother disembarked in Germany.

Documents for my mother showed that soldiers took her to Stutthof after her boat journey. It seems likely police took Helēna and Kazimirs there so that camp officials could treat them for their typhoid.[2] Confinement lasted two to four weeks, during which time, prisoners did not work. After camp officials treated Helēna and Kazimirs, they could have assigned them to other camps.

Solomeja's Path of Persecution

Solomeja went to four German concentration camps in a period of eight months. It was common for officials to transfer prisoners to a series of camps within a short period of time. Nazis moved one of the most famous prisoners, Anne Frank, three times in as many months. They took her to Westerbork transit camp in Holland in August 1944, then Auschwitz in September, and finally Bergen-Belsen in October.[3]

None of my mother's documents explained why she was moved so often. Her first two evacuations were due to Russian troops advancing on the towns where she was being held. Likewise, Russian maneuvers in Estonia possibly ended her month-long stay at Stutthof camp. Germans brought their Estonian prisoners from the Klooga concentration camp to the Stutthof camp when Soviets took Nazi-occupied Estonia in August 1944.[4]

Both the Germans and the Russians kept files on my mother's wartime movements. The International Tracing Service (ITS) provided German logs tracing her movements from August 15, 1944, to November 29, 1944.[5] The NKVD documents covered her transfers from March 13, 1944, through December 30, 1946.[6]

The ITS file reported that the Sipo (Sicherheitspolizel/Security Police) shipped my mother out from Rīga Harbor on August 15, 1944, and placed her in Stutthof concentration camp (current-day Sztutowo). Officials then sent her to Neuengamme camp on September 13, where she remained until November 29, 1944, which is when her record ends.

Stutthof[7] was the first Nazi concentration camp built on Polish soil and the last to be dissolved. The camp was located in a secluded, wet, and wooded area west of the small town of Stutthof, twenty-one miles east of Gdansk, Poland. An electrified barbed wire fence surrounded the camp containing thirty barracks that held prisoners from Czechoslovakia, Estonia, Hungary, Poland, and Latvia.

In its earliest years, Stutthof camp conducted immediate extermination of its prisoners, using mobile gas units. But by the summer of 1944, Germans stopped the practice of killing Jews, Romas, homosexuals, and political prisoners on arrival.

Germans had to handle the constant drain on their manpower, both on the battlefield and in their concentration camps. They were caught up in an endless cycle of replacing fallen soldiers and workers in their camps with prisoners from their occupied territories. In the final year, as the number of foreign male workers died from the inhumane conditions of the camps, they brought in larger numbers of women.

Knowing my mother was one of the camp's forced laborers was in itself hard to accept. But it was the written accounts detailing the humiliating entry process for female inmates that became painful. As I read about what women experienced in their admission process, I had to wonder how that shame aggravated her deteriorating mental state.

Female guards at Stutthof followed a carefully scripted drill for newly arrived female prisoners in the Old Camp square. The entry process for inmates took a whole day or even longer, regardless of the weather. Guards beat the prisoners before they registered them. They ordered prisoners to strip on the camp square and turn over all personal possessions for use in the camp stores.[8]

Head shearing and shaving followed. Officers told inmates the procedure prevented lice. Concern for health was only one reason Germans had for taking hair from inmates. Soldiers used disinfected hair for boots the guards wore, packed it in the mattresses inmates slept on, made hair-yarn socks for U-boat crews, and used it as industrial felt.

But hair removal brought about something far worse in psychological terms. It was a deliberate effort to depersonalize and humiliate inmates, something that Nazis succeeded at doing for scores of prisoners, many of whom mentioned it as the most mortifying aspect of their time in the camps.

The final stage of the entry process was taking a cold shower, during which SS men yelled and beat the women. Inmates received camp clothing made out of old rags. Guards gave them clogs, trousers, and a loose-fitting blouse made of some thin material.

Prisoners then reported to a clerk who recorded their personal details. Those details appeared on the *Haftlingskarte* (Prisoner's Personal Card). My mother's card stated my mother's drop-off location (*einlieferungsstelle*) was Rīga on August 15, 1944. The *Sipo*, shorthand for *Sicherheitspolizel*, *Security Police*, admitted her to the Stutthof concentration camp as inmate no. 63418. Her category was *Schtzhat, politsch*, or political prisoner.

Since my mother had a third-grade education and spoke no German, it is doubtful how much she understood during the intake interview. The only languages she knew were Latvian, Latgalian, and some Russian. The entry clerk used German spellings for her names (*Salomea* instead of Salomeja, and *Plataschs* instead of Platace). The same official entered her family name as *Danowskis* (rather than Danovskis) and entered *Andrupines* (instead of Andrupene) for her home.

The report was both revealing and concealing at the same time. Since I had no pictures of her, the words on the discolored piece of paper gave me a partial glimpse of what she looked like. I trained a magnifying glass on the German words describing different parts of her anatomy, but only a few letters and numbers were discernible.

With the online German-to-English translator and the help of a German friend, I began to make out my mother's height. It was (possibly) 1.59 meters. Two digits were clear: the 1 and a 9. The middle digit was harder to decipher. My German friend Marga guessed it looked like a 5, which meant my mother stood at 5 feet 2 inches, which was my adult height.

My mother's stature was "slim," and her eyes were blue. But the entries for hair, weight (*gewicht*), nose (*nase*), ears (*ohren*), and teeth (*zahne*) were unreadable. Several other categories—let alone what was written next to them—were smudged and therefore unreadable.

This level of detail on the physical features of every person reflected the German fixation on eugenics,[9] which was the basis for their effort at creating "the master race."

The entry clerk checked the box *verheiratet* for "married," followed by the name of my mother's *Ehemann* (husband), Broņislavs. The most revealing part of the report appeared next, the reason for her imprisonment: *Grund: als Geisel fur den Mann* (Reason: taken hostage for the husband).

Seeing my father's name and the reason for my mother's imprisonment made it official. The Germans singled her out for this "path of persecution," in the words of the ITS staff, because she was standing in for my father, who escaped the reach of the Nazis on March 13, 1944. What I don't know is whether the security police told her that.

If they told her, the seeds of her animosity against my father, already sown at Rēzekne Prison, quite possibly took firm root then.

There was one curious item. The box with the heading *Kinder* (children) had the number 1 that appeared on the line separating male and female. That seems to suggest there was no gender for my mother's child.

How could my mother report that she had one child whose gender was unknown? Might it have been that my mother knew enough German to say she had a child but didn't know the words for male or female? Then again, perhaps it was a case of careless form filling on the part of the clerk. Whatever the reason was, it was one more unanswered question about my mother.

Neuengamme Concentration Camp

On September 29, 1944, the commandant of the concentration camp at Stutthof presented the "takeover negotiations" for my mother. The Germans deported my mother, along with four hundred ninety-nine other female inmates, to Neuengamme concentration camp.[10] The ITS report showed that she stayed there at least two months. Then the trail runs cold. The person filing my mother's ITS report in August 2015 wrote to me:

> With regard to the further way of persecution or the further stay of your mother after 29th November 1944 there is not any information available in our archives. This unsatisfactory result is due to the fact that the documents preserved here are not complete. Many records were destroyed in the final phase of the Nazi regime.

Most prisoners at Neuengamme were political, punished for resisting the German occupation. The camp kept female inmates as laborers in twenty sub camps that spread out over northern Germany. They housed thirty-seven thousand female workers, representing a little over twenty percent of the ninety-six sub camps in 1944.

One-third of the women at that time worked for the Nazi war industry, performing in all weather, under the constant beatings of SS guards. Officials also assigned women to handle camp administration, its stores, and the kitchen. Since my mother had no special skills outside of farming, she may have worked in the kitchen, the kind of work prison officials assigned to her and Helēna in Rēzekne.

Bergen-Belsen Camp

Sometime after November 29, Germans sent my mother to Bergen-Belsen, often called Belsen. That is where the NKVD file picked up from where the ITS file left off. In that interrogation, my mother said she was at Belsen one month, which suggests she was held at Neuengamme for six months, even though she never mentioned that camp in her interrogations.

I speculated about my mother's suspected pregnancy during her time in the three concentration camps. If she were pregnant, there could have been any one of three outcomes. She could have miscarried, Germans killed the baby at birth, or it died a short time after its birth. Miscarriages happened frequently in the hostile environments of the camps, and newborns had a low survival rate in the camps.

Germans brutalized children as well as adults. They killed most children, Jewish or not, on arrival. Even if my mother's baby had escaped detection, it would have succumbed to pneumonia, the chief killer for most babies born in a concentration camp. The few children allowed to live in the camps became forced laborers or subjects of inhumane medical experiments.[11]

There were few female inmates who managed to hide their pregnancies (usually under the loose-fitting prison uniforms), gave birth to their babies, and hid them up through the time of their release from the camps. Mothers managed to recruit a team of other female inmates who took turns watching their infants as they carried out their assignments on different work shifts. Three famous Holocaust survivors from the Mauthausen concentration camp, all now seventy years old talked about being born in coal wagons or on a wooden plank on a factory floor.[12]

Bergen-Belsen camp was located in Lower Saxony in northern Germany.[13] The camp my mother entered in the spring of 1945 had become—even by concentration camp standards—unacceptably dirty and overcrowded. Designed originally to hold about ten thousand inmates, it held sixty thousand in February 1945, which led to a typhus epidemic, the disease that took away Anne Frank and her sister just months after their arrival. Starvation, diarrhea, and tuberculosis were also killing people faster than guards could bury them.

As I read what the entry process was like for women at Bergen-Belsen, the same revulsion I had reading about the intake process at Stutthof came over me when reviewing the Belsen accounts. They were even more graphic than the ones for Stutthof.

There were male and female *kapos*,[14] prisoners employed as guards and assistants, who shaved not only the heads of females but pubic hair as well. Then the *kapos* took off my mother's clothes and held her down while another woman inspected all her natural bodily openings.

This degrading process continued as women were later forced to parade around naked and bald in front of male prison guards. The intention was clear: break down a woman's spirit by making insulting remarks about her and instill fear into the group she was in.[15]

While no record states the reason Germans sent my mother to Belsen, the history of the camp suggests Nazis could have sent her there for at least two reasons. The camp took political prisoners and the overflow of female inmates from Neuengamme camp. It also had a recovery program (*Erholungslager*) for ill prisoners. My mother met the first two conditions. By the time she entered in March 1945, the camp had received around nine thousand women and young girls.

The third reason Belsen accepted women was because it had a recovery program (*Erholungslager*) for ill prisoners. It is doubtful my mother went to its recovery program to deal with health issues, because she told the NKVD interrogator she was at Belsen only one month, didn't work in the camp, and was released in April by English forces.

That meant she was among the 1,200 "healthy" women whom soldiers evacuated from the camp on April 24 and 25. Still, before the British released them, workers deloused them before sending them to a nearby Panzer army camp and later to other displaced persons camps.[16]

Helēna's Path of Persecution

Helēna talked about two concentration camps. She mentioned Königsberg (present-day Kaliningrad) to her daughter, Leonora; she named Ravensbrück to her grandson, Juris Sorokins. [17] It's possible she was at both camps. Nazis moved thousands of prisoners around on a frequent basis for a variety of reasons, my mother and Anne Frank being just two such individuals.

Helēna's failure to mention both camps to her family could have been the result of the disorientation she and so many other prisoners experienced in Germany. Being transferred to several camps by armed guards in a strange country whose language she didn't speak could have easily clouded her memory, especially since she was a woman who had relatively little formal education.

Helēna's description of Königsberg is a case in point. Facts on record do not support what she said about it. She talked about meeting American women there and said the British liberated her camp. While there was a camp at Königsberg, it held American POWs, not foreign prisoners brought in as laborers.

Her camp had no American women, only Europeans. There were Danish prisoners, some of whom might have spoken English to her, leading her to conclude they were American.

She might have been at Stutthof concentration camp. The main camp, Stutthof, was a good distance—ninety-one miles—from Königsberg. But if one looks at the camp's configuration at the time Helēna arrived in Germany, she had reason to believe she was at Königsberg. In September 1944, Germans established sub camps to house the growing number of forced laborers who kept Germany's war machine running. The camps around Stutthof began to proliferate and spread out for miles.

There were forty-one sub camps that Stutthof ran, including two sub camps set up for female prisoners. Those camps were located about thirty miles from Königsberg. One of them was Schippenbeil camp (current-day Sępopol), located in the region of Bartosyce, which borders Kaliningrad Oblast.[18]

What seems likely is that after Helēna was quarantined at the main camp at Stutthof, officials sent her to one of its satellite camps located on the outskirts of Königsberg. Guards could have mentioned the nearby city to the inmates on several occasions. Prisoners had only the guards to inform them about their location.

Her statement—that British soldiers liberated her camp—is harder to explain, because whether she was at Stutthof or Ravensbrück in April 1945, the British did not liberate either camp. The Russians did.

Could she and other inmates have mistakenly assumed the Allies were either British or American? Even though Russia was one of the four Allies, Helēna's memory of Russia's reign of terror during the Terrible Times could have disqualified them in her mind as a group that was liberating her and others. And it's impossible to know if she made that conclusion on her own or was simply repeating what her fellow inmates said.

Her one plausible memory was that soldiers took her and other freed inmates into the abandoned flats of a nearby city to take some nice clothing left behind by fleeing Germans. If she were in one of the two sub camps that Stutthof ran, it was only thirty miles from Konigsberg. That trip into the city is perhaps the reason why she remembered the city's name.

The camp for which she gave a name, Ravensbrück, was near Fürstenberg, on the picturesque banks of Lake Schwedt in the Oberhavel district. It was a women's concentration camp where 130,000 to132,000 female prisoners passed through its system from 1939 to 1945. Its inmates came from all occupied countries.[19]

There were seventy sub camps used for slave labor. Many women worked in the camp as employees of the German electrical engineering company of Siemens and Halske. My grandmother would have worn a color-coded triangle denoting her nationality. Polish women wore red triangles; common criminals wore green triangles; prostitutes, Gypsies, lesbians, or women who refused to marry wore black triangles.

It's likely she wore a blue triangle, which was set aside for foreign workers whose nationality could not be established due possibly to the breakdown in recordkeeping. Australian journalist Louise Adler said that by late 1944, when Helēna might have been there,[20]

> Order was crumbling under the sheer number of victims to be worked to death, exterminated or sent on death marches to other camps. The Third Reich's efficient record-keeping gave way to chaos and method gave way to panic as defeat became inevitable.

It's doubtful that guards shaved Helēna's hair. Unlike Stutthof and Belsen, where every laborer went through the head-shearing process, only Czech and Polish women had to undergo that procedure at Ravensbrück. Guards spared Scandinavian women, particularly Norwegian women, since Nazis viewed them as the one group having the most Aryan features, starting with their blue eyes and blond hair.

While there is no mention of women from Baltic countries, it is likely Helēna was grouped with Scandinavian women, since she had blue eyes and—if not blond hair—at least light-colored hair. She was fifty-four years old, so she had light, thinning gray hair.

Helēna recalled that she was in C-campus, where she slept on bare wood shelves and ate soup made from potato skins and water. Her most vivid memory was female camp guards constantly yelling "Appell, appell!" at roll call. It was the daily routine when prisoners had to sometimes stand for upwards of four hours, both at morning and at night.[21]

Helēna remembered guards who used whips that gave her sharp shooting pains. One of them could have been Irma Grese, whom one inmate described as a person who "swaggered at the camp with a pistol strapped to her waist and a whip in her hand."[22]

Despite the daily atrocities and hardships women endured on a daily basis, there were small and personal victories they created for themselves. They shared recipes, formed music groups, had a theater, even had a secret newspaper. They held history or language classes, where, perhaps, some of the Scandinavians taught English, which could have led Helēna to believe they were Americans.[23]

Helēna also exploited one special skill to her advantage, telling people their fortunes. Making prophecies was a childhood game for her, something she was quite good at doing. But it was not until she saw its value in the camp that she maximized its potential for survival.

It started soon after she entered her camp, when she predicted a particular guard at the camp would get shot. To everyone's amazement, he was shot the very next day. A partisan sniper from outside the camp fired into the camp, trying to free the inmates.

The partisan failed in that regard, but the news of the guard's death launched Helena's camp career as a fortune-teller. Even some guards asked her to read their fortunes. She did not read palms but worked with nearby objects such as a piece of bread.

If she had been at Ravensbrück when it was liberated, she would have faced one of two possible endings. If she were one of the three thousand ill or dying prisoners, soldiers would have left her behind. But if she were in reasonably good physical condition, she would have joined twenty-four thousand women who were ordered to go on a death march out of the camp.

Germans had two reasons for this evacuation procedure, which they used in a number of camps. They wanted no live witnesses left behind to testify against them, and they expected prisoners to die during the grueling march that would go on for more than a hundred miles.

Soldiers led women out from their district of Oberhavel, where Ravensbrück camp was, to the region of Mecklenburg. No records indicated which town in Mecklenburg soldiers took the women. The closest town to Fürstenberg was Schwerin—155 miles away. The furthest was Neubrandenburg, 205 miles. But reaching a destination was not the goal of the march; death was the sole purpose of doing it. Russian scouts sent by the Red Army troops liberated the survivors at some point in their march.

I do not think Helēna was on the death march to Mecklenburg. The most plausible path the Nazis sent my grandmother on during her eight months in Germany seems to be her confinement at Stutthof to treat her typhoid, then her transfer to Ravensbrück, and finally back to Stutthof. Berlin was the closest city of any size outside of Ravensbrück—seventy-five miles away—where Russian soldiers could have taken her and other inmates to find clothing left behind. But she never mentioned Berlin; the only German city that was fixed in her mind was Königsberg.

Kazimirs's Path of Persecution

The surviving daughter of Kazimirs, Zinaīda, didn't know the name of his camp but gave some clues about it. His ability to survive the subhuman conditions of his camp was that guards used him as a tailor. He repaired and made their uniforms, for which they provided him with a Singer sewing machine. The double irony is that while his act of mending Soviet parachutes led to his arrest by the Germans, those tailoring skills kept him from a slow and certain death in his camp.

But as much as the Germans valued his skills as a tailor, he was still vulnerable to the mercurial acts of some junior officers in the camp. Inmates were shot without notice and for no reason at all. At one point, Kazimirs came into disfavor with one guard, who ordered him to be shot.

As he was sitting in a room, waiting for death, a general saw him and asked, "What are you doing here, Platačs?" That kind of familiarity he had with the military brass, who knew him by name, suggested he had standing with the camp officials. Whatever the offense was that Kazimirs had committed, a military commander countermanded the overzealous order of some subordinate. They were not about to eliminate the man who made and repaired their military uniforms.

His daughter, Zinaīda, provided one clue about his camp. Americans liberated it. If one restricts the possible camps to the ones that had a large number of German officers, and which were liberated by American troops, Kazimirs could have been in one of seven camps.

A likely camp was the Dora-Mittelbau (also known as Dora-Nordhausen or Nordhausen). It was in central Germany near the southern Harz Mountains, north of the town of Nordhausen. In October 1944, the time Kazimirs might have been sent there, the SS made Dora-Mittelbau an independent concentration camp with more than thirty sub camps of its own.[24]

Days before Allied troops marched on his camp in 1945, he came down again with a bad case of typhus. The Germans found him too weak to send him to Bergen-Belsen or to go on their death march, which killed thousands of inmates. Americans found him just in time to treat him.

Solomeja, Helēna, and Kazimirs survived the mentally and physically crippling conditions of their camps due a number of factors. One was fortuitous timing, arriving at their camps in the final months of the Third Reich. My grandmother and great-uncle demonstrated a strength and resilience that were bolstered by a strong desire to return to their families. They went back to Latvia on trains the Allies provided to them in the spring of 1945.

Helēna and Kazimirs had the strength and the temperament to overcome their devastating internment. Leonora said that while her mother wasn't the prettiest of women, she endured by being sturdy, helpful, and wise. Kazimirs could have derived additional power and a sense of dignity, since he was able to use his professional skills as a tailor.

Solomeja fared less well. While she survived physically, the emotional and psychological disarray she experienced ran so deep that she did not want to return to Latvia. She stayed on in Germany another eighteen months.

What my mother might have looked like at
age twenty-one, myself at that age
The *Fremont Tribune*, Fremont, Nebraska, April 1, 1965

Great-Uncle Kazimirs with his sewing machine and accordion
Photo from Leonora Platace's family album

CHAPTER 7

Rīga Orphanage

The Little Inhabitants of Kapseļu Street

WHEN LAURIS PRESENTED the copy of my record at Rīga Orphanage, its size alone impressed me. It measured sixteen and a half inches by eleven and a half inches. The information it gave not only provided an amazing array of detail on my physical condition but also spoke of other issues related to my background and the politics of the time.

The tag around my neck at Salaspils camp gave my name, birth date, and hometown. My name (*bērna uzvārds un vārds*) was Platačs Marija. My date of birth (*dzimis*) was May 30, 1943, and my home (*Reģistrets*) was Andrupene, a region (*pagasts*) of the city of Rēzekne. All other information came from the soldiers who brought me to the one childcare institution in Rīga.[1]

Latvia's first president, Jānis Čakste, opened the orphanage, the oldest Latvian childcare center, in 1922 as the National Infant Shelter. Through the years, its functions and location on Kapseļu Street have remained the same. Its name would change four times: Rīga City Infant House, Rīga Republican Mental Infant House, and Orphan Care Center "Rīga." Since 1994, it has been called the National Social Care Center, Rīga Branch.

Platačs Marija, No. 3072

On September 2, 1944, the clerk at the Rīga Orphanage entered me as no. 3072.[2] My orphanage records showed that as I entered, I was not well fed. There were parasite bite marks and small blue spots on my skin. I had a reddish throat. There was something about the feet, which Lauris found was unreadable. But otherwise, my health was developing "normally." Glands, heart, lungs, liver, and spleen were normal. Latvian entries on two lung X-rays showed "negative" or "normal" results.

Monthly checkups appeared on my weight, head circumference, and length. In the Illnesses column, there were notations on vaccinations. Staff listed checkups for a range of diseases (*slimības*), which included tuberculosis (*tuberkulozes*), typhus (*tīfs*), and the grippe, an old fashioned term for influenza.

Eugenics

The staff measured my health and growth, which they were to do with meticulous care in the years that followed. As for the Germans, the "barons" from whom the Latvian caretakers took their orders, the reason they brought me into the orphanage was because I had two characteristics they cared about most: the color of my eyes (*acu krāsa*), which were blue (*zila*), and the color of my hair (*matu krāsa*), which was blond (*blonda*).

Even though the Lebensborn Association was winding down alongside Germany's military losses, Nazis were still admitting children to orphanages that fit a certain profile, the first two characteristics being the more obvious ones. I was one of eight infants whom soldiers delivered to the orphanage. Our ages ranged from sixteen to twenty-four months.

It is unknown whether orphanage staff knew that any of this was going on. What did they know or suspect about the circumstances of the children coming from Salaspils? Did they know that Germans separated us from our parents because they were branded as dissidents? Did the staff know that parents such as my mother were either killed at Salaspils or sent to concentration camps?

It is pure speculation. One thing the staff knew for certain. They had no choice but to write what the soldiers told them to write on each of us they kidnapped, even if they suspected much of it was false. The first was my legitimacy.

The incoming clerk wrote the Latvian word *māte* (mother) in the space for my parents' names and also the word ārlaulības (illegitimate). The clerk might have wondered about that but had no way to question it. The soldiers gave the reason for being admitted (*ievietošanas iemesls*): "no parents, brought by Germans, separated from the mother, sent to Germany" (*bērns no mātes, kura nosūtīta uz Vāciju, atņemts*). Since my parents' names were unknown, and I had no known relatives, the orphanage accepted me.

Two other entries struck me as unusual. There was a psychological test and an examination of my genital area. There were no dates next to them, and no explanation why or how they were done. The word *normal* appeared next to Psychological Assessment. The notation "no vaginal discharge" appeared all by itself.

I wondered, why would the staff conduct these exams on an infant or toddler? Then I learned these kinds of exams were routine for children seized by Nazis for their Lebensborn Association. It all went in lockstep with the Third Reich's emphasis on eugenics.

A thorough internal and psychological examination ensured the rigorous inspection that Nazis required of all its children. None could have any "defects." Every aspect of a child's physical and psychological being had to conform to their notions of a perfect Aryan individual.

This focus on eugenics was not just Hitler's exclusive domain. It was part of an international phenomenon that predated World War II, a topic of study that originated in America. The interest in every aspect of a person's psychological and physical makeup played right into the German program of creating its "master race," one that was racially pure, which extended right down to children.

Gitta Sereny, a child welfare officer with the United Nations Relief and Rehabilitation Agency in 1946, wrote about the role eugenics played in the countries of Eastern Europe and the Balkans while she was working in the US zone of Germany after the war. She reported how Nazis kidnapped many thousands of children and replaced Germany's own population with "racially valuable children." The children they seized had to meet certain specifications, which were extensive.

The Office for Race and Settlement that Nazis established decided the children's suitability for germanization on the basis of measurements of sixty-two parts of their bodies. Sereny described the selection process for children taken to orphanages the Germans ran in occupied countries such as Latvia:[3]

> The decisive characteristics for being placed in the top racial categories, aside from a child's hair and eye color, were the shape of the nose and lips, the hairline, and the toe and fingernails, and the condition of the genitalia. Important too were reactions to neurological tests, and personal habits: Persistent uncleanliness and, of course, bedwetting, farting, nail-biting, and masturbation—which older boys were told on arrival was forbidden—were, if repeatedly observed, automatic disqualifications.

Jānis Riekstiņš, a Latvian writer, and himself a war orphan (having spent five years at Naukšēni orphanage), has written extensively about Latvian orphans. He wrote about the record keeping at Rīga's orphanage in a periodical:[4]

> To learn the many decades long history of Rīga Orphanage, the tragic and complicated fates of its little inhabitants, one doesn't need to go to the big archives and search through the orphan cases. You can see it in the orphanage itself, where the laughter, cries, and also calls for helps were heard every day. All children are scrupulously documented, the documents tell which were adopted by relatives, transferred to other orphanages, fallen sick, or died . . . year after year.

Dr. Bergfelde

I first learned that I was one of Rīga Orphanage's "little inhabitants" in 1963. A classmate at the university who wished to write an article about my Latvian roots asked me to find out what I could about my parents.

MARIJA PLATACE FUTCHS FINE

My German professor suggested that she would help me write to the mayor of Hahnenklee, where I spent five years in the Rīga Orphanage in Germany (as it was called by many in the Latvian community during the war). He responded, giving me several leads.

The most promising contact was a Latvian lady living in Australia, Dace Darzins. She wrote on behalf of her aunt, whose name appeared as Dr. V. Bergfelds, the director of the Rīga Orphanage during the time I was there. She answered me by writing,[5]

> Having no records—as they were left at the orphanage at the time the doctor left in August 1947—she remembers, however, the following about you: Marija Platačs is a legitimate child whose mother died in childbirth and whose father at that time was at the front fighting against the communists. Therefore the baby was admitted to the Rīga orphanage. (Platačs in translation means "wide eyes.") Dr. V. Bergfelds does not recall any living relatives, only that the Platačs family came from the Andrupene county (Andrupienes pagasts), which is situated in the eastern part of Latvia called Latgale. In the latter years, i.e., 1946–1947 Marija was an intelligent, industrious and sympathetic girl. That is all that Dr. V. Bergfelds can recall from memory.

Until I reopened the search for my parents' identities in 2014, I had no reason to question Dr. Bergfelde's recollections. Receiving her niece's letter was more than I could have hoped for at that time, especially when Soviets barred overseas Latvians from finding out who their parents and relatives were.

The niece had the foresight to say Dr. Bergfelde had no access to orphanage records and so was drawing on what she remembered about me. I was, after all, one of dozens of orphans in her charge. The doctor did, in fact, mix me up with another child. I doubt that was deliberate prevarication on her part. Without orphanage records at hand, she relied as best as she could on a memory that had faded after more than a decade.

That would be one of two accounts she gave about me. There was an official document she signed in 1948 that described my status. It again included false information and raised questions about what she said in her niece's 1963 letter. I would learn about that document quite by chance in 2015.

The initial number of fifty orphans in September 1944 expanded to seventy-six orphans a month later. Once again, Russians forced Germans to move us as they closed in to take Rīga. Germans transferred us to a school in the seaside town of Swinemunde (now Świnoujście, Poland), over six hundred miles to the south of Rīga. It seemed to be a safe place, though events would prove otherwise.

Entrance to Riga Orphanage, August 2014
(now the National Social Care Center, Rīga Branch)
Photo by Marija Platace Futchs Fine

The Midland, Midland University, Fremont, Nebraska
February 1, 1963

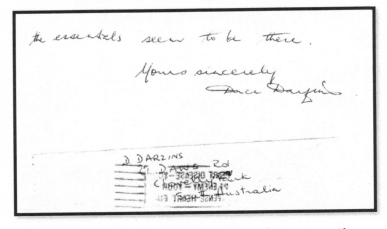

12/6/63

Dear Manya Futchs,

When I received your letter, I forwarded it to my aunt, Dr. V. Bergfelds, who has been the principal of the Riga Orphanage for quite a long time. Unfortunately she has no documents of the children with her because they were all left at the orphanage when she resigned in August 1947. She remembers, however, the following about you:

Manya Platais is a legitimate child whose mother died in childbirth and whose father at that time was at the front fighting against the communists; therefore the baby was admitted to the Riga orphanage. (Platais in translation means "wide eyes".) Dr. V. Bergfelds does not recall any living relatives, only that the Platais family came from the Andrupiene county (Andrupienes pagasts) which is situated in the eastern part of Latvia called Latgale. In the latter years, i.e. 1946-47 Manja was an intelligent, industrious and sympathetic girl. That is all that Dr. V. Bergfelds can recall from memory.

I am sorry that I cannot furnish you with any other facts but the essentials seem to be there.

Yours sincerely
Dace Darzins

D. DARZINS
Australia

Letter from Dace Darzins, niece of Dr. Veronika Bergfelds, on December 6, 1963, written in response to my inquiry for the article in the *The Midland*

CHAPTER 8

Swinemunde

My Heart Couldn't Bear
Leaving the Children

AS SOVIET TROOPS gained ground in Latvia in the late summer of 1944, orphanages in Rīga, Jūrmala, Liepāja,[1] and Baldone began to evacuate their staff and children. As Soviet troops stood ready to capture Rīga, the German "barons" ordered staff at the orphanages in Rīga and Majori to gather up nearly three hundred of us to set out for Swinemunde, now Świnoujście, Poland.

We faced a treacherous, uncertain journey with scarce resources. Lack of food supplies prompted some Majori caretakers to go to an island in Rīga, to work for a few kilos of potatoes. They also went begging for bread at a nearby soldier's bakery, where they managed to get only two bags of flour, by no means enough to feed hundreds of mouths.

Farmers were leaving, which meant, for Majori caretaker Alma Seķe, "death from starvation for us."[2] But farmers were not the only ones taking flight. The director of Majori Orphanage left, urging Alma to do the same. Two other officials walked away from what they called a too dangerous an undertaking.

One caretaker put it bluntly, "If the government refuses responsibility for the children, then you can't ask it from the employees." Alma was the only person willing to assume the role of leading Majori's 134 orphans to safety in Germany. While she shared the dread and fear others had for taking on such a responsibility, she said, "My heart couldn't bear leaving the children, with the same little heart beating in their chest, them wanting to live as much as we did."

Journey to Swinemunde

How ironic it is to realize the same Germans who had jailed my family in prisons and concentration camps were now clearing our way to safety because it was the Allied bombers who were bearing down on us. I was not yet seventeen months old, still not able to walk, so adults would be taking turns carrying me and others along the way.

Alma Seķe headed up the Majori group, with nearly a dozen Latvian caretakers supporting her. Dr. Veronika Bergfelde was in charge of the one hundred forty-eight of us from Rīga Orphanage, with twenty-eight staff members joining her.

Alma provided the gripping narrative of what transpired on our journey. She showed exemplary toughness and admirable resourcefulness as she took on the responsibility of shepherding her charges.

As I studied her image (p 91 in this book), I could see that she had a penetrating gaze, well suited for keeping focus on the difficult task at hand. Her hair was parted straight down the middle with a plaited headband wrapped around the back of her head, forming what some might call the halo or crown top.

From the outset, Alma showed the toughness and resolve she was to demonstrate over the next few months. She worked with any powerful or resourceful individual she could find on behalf of the children. She explained,

> So I went to Rīga to meet Mr Niedra, the head of the evacuation committee, and General Rūdolfs Bangerskis,[3] asking to take us to Kurzeme to save our lives. Because seeing German reinforcements in Jūrmala, one could guess we would be in the line of fire. That day I didn't get any clarity, only a promise we will be helped. I asked General Bangerskis for his photograph, choosing one where he is in his uniform, thinking it might help me in the future. A few days passed and our situation worsened. On the afternoon of October 3, I got a call from some official who said that tomorrow, October 4, we will be driven to Rīga and then

to Germany. It was Mr Bangerskis and then-director of
National Help, Mr. Adolfs Silde, who got the buses for us.

As Soviets marched into Rīga on October 4, the orphanage staff
took all of us out to Rīga Harbor to set sail on the cargo steamship
Minder Bremen for Gotenhafen, modern-day Gdynia Harbor—Poland's
"window on the world."

Alma inspected our ship and found it dirty. She called General
Bangerskis several times, trying to get the Rīga and Majori orphans
something better, perhaps an infirmary ship. That ended when a car
pulled up with two men in it. The driver called out that his passenger
was a German general, who told Alma, "If you don't want to go on this
ship, you can go back. Believe me, there is no space on other ships."

Together with Dr. Bergfelde, the women inspected the rooms on
board. They were not the best, but both decided that if they covered
the floors with mattresses, everyone could settle in.

General Bangerskis continued to involve himself in his helpful
manner. On the evening of October 4, he brought sweets, two boxes
of butter, a bag of sugar, semolina, and oat flakes. A representative of
a national Latvian help agency, National Assistance, brought a warm
dinner for the caretakers and lunch for the next day.

As I researched the movements my mother and I made after our
separation in Salaspils, I calculated the distance between the cities that
separated us over the next four years. In this instance, I was within two
months of being in the same Rīga shipyard as my mother. She left on
August 15; we were there on October 4.

Thirty Latvian children from another orphanage joined us at the
dock in Rīga Harbor. They were from Baldone, a town twenty miles
west of Rīga. Their arrival presented an immediate medical threat, as
they had scabies. They contracted the disease from having been cooped
up in a basement with German soldiers to avoid bombing raids. The
skin disease then spread to some of the others in our group.

After the boat arrived in Gdynia, all of us boarded a train for
the 207-mile journey to Swinemunde. But as Alma was to observe in
retrospect,

We were wrong to think that our troubles will end upon arrival. I could barely stand when the ship anchored, but that was nothing compared to what began (after that).

Swinemunde Orphanage

The 246 of us arrived in Swinemunde on October 8, 1944. The port of Swinemunde on the Isle of Usedom lies one and a half miles above the mouth of the river Swine from which it received its name. Located on the Baltic Sea and Stettin Lagoon, it was an important shipping center on two major islands from which many smaller ones fanned out into the sea.[4]

In WWII, Swinemunde's islands were swarming with refugees. When we arrived on October 8, 1944, the city, whose prewar population was twenty-two thousand, had swelled up to one hundred thousand. It was, as one observer described it, "filled to bursting with frantic, half-starved, and exhausted refugees from East Prussia and Pomerania." They were escaping Russians in their horse drawn carriages or by ships filling the harbor and waiting their turn to disembark their human cargo.[5]

More than two hundred of us scattered to several surrounding towns. The Liepāja orphans went to Mecklenburg in the northeastern part of Germany. My Rīga group settled in Swinemunde, and Majori orphans went to Ahlbeck, three miles from us.

The Majori group reported to a German orphanage whose supervisor was a German woman, Frau Butow. The caretakers of Rīga orphans took us children to an abandoned school in Swinemunde. In the coming months, four more children joined us, three Latvians and one Estonian, which brought our total up to one hundred fifty-two children.

Alma and Dr. Bergfelde talked often with each other over the next six months about sharing medicines and supplies. Since there was no public means of transportation, staff from each orphanage walked between the two adjoining towns to handle many issues, chief among them meeting our medical needs.

Tempers flared between the principal caretakers over medical treatments and food resources at the two orphanages. Alma attempted to bring in Dr. Bergfelde, a trained medical doctor, to treat the children in Ahlbeck. Frau Butow rejected that out of hand.

She called in a German doctor instead, who made only occasional visits. This created an ongoing feud between Dr. Bergfelde and Alma over who could give Majori children shots. Because Frau Butow's doctor was often unavailable to do it, and Dr. Bergfelde was barred from giving injections, Alma took matters into her own hands.

Being the proactive individual she was, she volunteered to sterilize the needles and give injections herself to the children. Dr. Bergfelde warned her that even if she took those precautionary measures, it could lead to her arrest. Alma responded by saying she didn't worry about herself, gave the injections, and reported, "Thank God. I did well." The Germans never arrested her.

We were all in constant need of medicines. Alma wrote that she spent one hundred reichmarks[6] (US$249) on medicines at one point. She even persuaded Dr. Bergfelde to allow Alma to write her own name on prescriptions since she didn't have time to go to an apothecary in Swinemunde. All she brought with her were the limited supply of vitamins and medicines she carried from Latvia.

Just as the scarcity of food was an issue at the beginning of the trip, it continued to be one in Swinemunde. Alma and Frau Butow came to blows over how to measure out limited amounts of food. She did not want the sick children receiving the same portions as the healthy ones.

The German orphanage director wanted to give the ill ones a mixture of glume flour with water. Alma flared up, saying that in Latvia that was what they used as glue for wallpaper. Frau Butow screamed back, saying Alma's insolence would land her in a concentration camp, a term Alma had heard but didn't know what it meant.

She apologized, saying she didn't know how else to call the brew Frau Butow had in mind. Once she apologized, Alma was able to convince Frau Butow to use the semolina and porridge provided by General Bangerskis.

Requests Dr. Bergfelde made to the Swedish Red Cross and other groups were rebuffed. One was the Latvian Committee in Berlin. The other was the National Socialist People Welfare (NSP), a social welfare organization during the Third Reich established in 1933 and was headquartered in Berlin.

Even though both women labored under the uncertainty and turmoil of war, they still maintained the daily schedule their orphanages followed in Latvia. Alma gave the daily schedule of the Majori orphans, which was probably the same for us in Swinemunde.

At 6:00 a.m. the staff awakened us and tidied our rooms. At 7:00 a.m. caretakers dressed us, cleaned out our potties, made our beds, washed the floors, and provided breakfast. At 8:00 a.m. we sat at tables, drawing letters and numbers.

Lunch was at noon. But, as Alma described the food, it was "simply put, horrid." Staff drank bitter black coffee. Children did not get the monthly requirement of eight hundred grams of sugar. The bread slices, reported Alma, "were so thin you could see through them."

The only natural foods available were kohlrabi, turnips, and cabbage leaves. The daily allotment per individual was four potatoes with vinegar, bran sauce, but no spices. Alma saw the basement in Frau Butow's orphanage brimming over with potatoes. But Frau was stingy with the number of potatoes she allowed. Alma wrote, "Every day I had to fight to get an extra potato or a cup of milk for the children."

At 1:00 p.m. the staff put us down for a nap, while other caretakers ran to the mail and pharmacy. At 2:00 p.m. staff took us out for a walk (weather permitting) and cut our hair.

At 6:00 p.m. staff gave us dinner, bathed us, and applied medications to those of us who were sick. The bathing ritual had to be meted out sparingly. Staff at Ahlbeck brought an iron bathtub into Alma's room and warmed up the water by pouring pitchers and buckets of water into it. Staff bathed two children each night. With 134 children, that meant a child got a bath once every two months.

At 7:00 p.m. staff put us down for the night, but the work for the staff continued, all of it related to handling our clothing. Laundry detail became a daily, labor-intensive ordeal, since clothing could not be sent out. Alma had already tried that, with disastrous results. The one time she sent out the children's clothes to a sailor's laundry, the wash came back wet and more dirty, so she and one other caretaker took over the laundry.

This routine would go on from about 7:00 p.m. until 10:00 p.m. or 11:00 p.m., which meant doing it in the dark as there was no electricity. Staff took advantage of the dark to rest a few hours and then commenced with washing clothes when electricity came on again, usually between 2:00 and 4:00 a.m.

Alma and the other caretakers used that time to mend old clothing or sew new togs. The manual labor and harsh detergents they used doing the laundry meant their "hands were bleeding; so [they] washed them with lysoform."

The staff would catch a few hours of sleep. "And then," Alma wrote, "it would start all over again." Throughout all these days, weeks, and months, our caretakers kept a faithful record of every single child's growth: our weight, our height, the circumference of our heads, and our illnesses.

Allied Bombings

In March 1945, the war came to Swinemunde, which the writer Jānis Riekstiņš described:[7]

> We must remember that Allies were fervently bombing German cities, so little Latvian orphans were facing real danger. And if they lived through it, it was due to the caretakers who were always with the children taking care of them.

In rude contrast to the admirable self-sacrificing activities of our caretakers, Frau Butow's behavior remained self-serving to the end. Alma wrote that the German director and her friends, the NVS "Leiters," [8] didn't want to let them go, because the Majori orphans and caretakers were a good source of food for them.

On March 12, 1945, Swinemunde came under a ferocious and unrelenting air attack. The Russian army, positioned twelve miles away, asked the Americans to run a mission that involved nearly seven hundred bombers. They unleashed 1,609 tons of bombs on the key German coastal town.[9]

Even though bombs destroyed intended military targets—a factory, several warehouses, and three transport ships—the human toll was even greater. It is estimated that between 5,000 and 23,000 persons lost their lives in this destructive raid. People called it the Dresden of the North.[10] Military analysts placed this bombing as the sixth-worst bombing campaign of WWII, the others being Osaka, Kassel, Darmstadt, Pforzheim, London, Berlin, Dresden, Hamburg, and Tokyo.

Dr. Bergfelde summed up the situation in a letter to the Swedish Latvian community: "There were alarms sounding every night. Then we were bombed and two weeks stuck in the basement, until the German Lords found it possible to release us."

Mr. Silde, director of National Help, arrived from Rīga and rounded us up to return to the habitable floors in the bombed-out school, where we had just enough time to prepare to leave for safer ground, the Harz Mountains[11] in northern Germany. Mr. Šilde sent Mr. Raudzins, the director of the Social Department of Latvian Orphanages, to guide us into the mountains with six additional caretakers.

Swinemunde, the town we had called home for nearly half a year changed from German to Soviet control. Russians renamed it Świnoujście on May 5, 1945. The Poles took control on October 6, 1945, and it has been a part of Poland ever since.

If we could make it, our final destination—Hahnenklee—promised freedom from bombings. Its forests gave dense cover to everything: houses, buildings, even an ammunitions factory the Germans safely hid from the Allies.

Hazardous Journey

Caretakers for the two orphanages set out on separate paths on different dates. Rīga orphans started out on March 27, 1945. Majori orphans began their journey a week later on April 7, 1945.

There is no account showing what route Rīga orphans took by train or how long it took. Alma and others, however, did document their journey. It gave a sense of the scale of horror that awaited the Majori orphans and their caretakers.

The more direct southern route was impassable. Berlin stood in the way. Russian troops had formed a ring around the city, just days before April 16, when Hitler's Third Reich collapsed.

Before the Majori group left, Alma gathered up reinforcements. Mr. Raudziņš, a Latvian Social Services official, and six caretakers arrived to help get the children out of Swinemunde. Alma and Raudziņš walked to Swinemunde from Ahlbeck, looking for ways to transport the children.

When they finally found a train, they made a mad dash as the children clutched onto their personal belongings in time to reach the train that was leaving for Harz Mountains in two hours. They literally ran from Swinemunde to the station as they dodged a rain of bombs and bullets. Francis Muhr,[12] regional consultant of Save the Children, wrote that Soviets bombed the train they were on, forcing them to get off the train, since children were very small with only a few caretakers.

Since they couldn't go directly to the Harz Mountains, they went in the opposite direction, eighty-six miles north, to Germany's largest isle, Rügen Island, situated off the Pomeranian coast on the Baltic Sea. The Majori orphans and their caretakers arrived at Promoisel, a village in the northernmost reaches of the island.

Every form of transport was out of reach. There were no boats or trains. Since they were in an agricultural area, Alma and the new director of Majori orphanage, Mr. Siliņš, went in search of wagons.

They walked back and forth multiple times from town to town, talking to farmers along the way. Just as it seemed their situation couldn't get any worse, it did. On April 29, Germans cut off the road leading off from the island.

Alma spoke to an army commander to see if they could get out, but he refused. In one day alone, Alma walked back and forth between towns, begging anyone she could find to take her charges off the island. The commander to whom she made one appeal did give orders to evacuate the children, only to have local German officials refuse to carry out the orders.

May 3 was the day of deliverance. Alma caught wind of a boat that was boarding in three hours. She begged a local farmer to give as many horses and carriages as he could provide to get the children and caretakers to the harbor.

She commandeered six carriages, which carried many of the children. The rest had to walk. But they were too late. Once all the carriages arrived at the harbor at Sassnitz, the ship had left.

Similar experiences occurred to other Latvian refugees whose memoirs I read. They recalled arriving too late for a bus, train, or boat, for which there were no posted schedules. They only learned about boats or trains leaving by word of mouth from passersby. Wartime provided no quick, safe exits.

There were also other memoirs that described unusually lucky experiences. A person or family had a chance meeting with a farmer on the road who carried them to a city in his wagon or on horseback. One writer even described the fortuitous occasion of standing on the railroad tracks when she heard a train coming down the track, not knowing where it was going, but boarding it, just to get out from under the bombs that were raining down all around them.

At 1:00 a.m. on May 3, Alma sought out a military commander in Sainz, pleading with him to get everyone on board a Danish ship, the *Hans Borge,* that was leaving in a few hours. The commander took her by one hand and held a gun in the other.

He told the captain of the *Hans Borge,* "If you don't let her and the children on your ship, I will shoot you right here." It worked. But they didn't want to repeat the disappointment of arriving too late as they had done earlier, so everyone left their belongings on shore.

Boarding started between 2:00 a.m. and 4:00 a.m. All during that time, explosions were going on from the sound of heavy Russian artillery. It was too much for Alma. As she recounted the event, she said, "I can't talk about it yet." She would never forget the night in Sassnitz.

By 8:00 a.m. on May 4, the ship left the harbor, just three hours before Russians conquered the city at 11:00 a.m. The *Hans Borge* headed for Denmark, but there were problems on arrival at Copenhagen. As Alma explained it, "the German lords wanted to continue to journey on to Germany but Danes asked to have their ship back."

The order to return the Danish ship was possibly part of Denmark's Jewish rescue operation. The country shipped over seven thousand of its Jews to nearby neutral Sweden using fishing boats, kayaks, ketches, regular ferries, and coastal freighters such as the *Hans Borge* for the one-hour journey.

By doing so, Denmark scaled one of the largest actions of collective resistance against Nazi Germany by using its ships. The result was that more than ninety-nine percent of Denmark's Jewish population avoided capture by the Nazis.[13]

Alma's group was stuck in Copenhagen for days, during which time she wrote letters appealing to the Danish Red Cross and other groups to send supplies. They found another ship on May 5 and journeyed on it until May 12. All during that time, Alma felt they were "like vagabonds on the ship."

The ship stopped in Kiel, Germany, where everyone boarded yet another boat, the *Linz*, by way of a big ladder that was fastened to a tiny ladder. It became a frightening logistical exercise. During the slow and arduous process of going from one ship to the other that night, Alma said, "God was with us and no one fell into the sea."

The *Linz* was a cargo ship whose crew was unhappy to see over a hundred souls crowded on the deck and below. Its small quarters were now strained to an unbearable breaking point. The crew placed the new arrivals in a storage room, where they laid themselves on shelves, on and under tables, as well as on the floor.

Alma brought in five electrical fans so children wouldn't suffocate, while caretakers slept outside on iron plates. There were four dried biscuits and a bit of canned meat for each person. Over two hundred persons had one bucket of water meant for just forty-eight people.

Even as the *Linz* pulled into Sierksdorf, Germany, the war raged all around the Majori group. Soldiers fired guns in every direction. After children and staff loaded themselves in wagons, bullets hit one cart, killing a couple of children and one caretaker.

Tragic though it was that gunfire took away two children, starvation and diseases ended the lives of thirty-eight children from October 1944 until the spring of 1945. Majori children finally arrived in Goslar, Germany, by train sometime late in May 1945, just as those of us from Rīga had arrived weeks earlier in April.

The Majori orphans split up into smaller groups, going to Sierksdorf, Hamburg, Malente, Fussau, Rolsdorff, Mussen, and Klinberg. We Rīga orphans had already gone en masse to Golf Hotel in Hahenklee.

It was an idyllic location, high in the hills, where the air was fresh and clear. During all that time, traveling under perilous conditions, Latvian caretakers continued to keep monthly records on our growth. In April 1945, one caretaker wrote "Stands" in the Development column on my record. Four months later, in August, there was another handwritten note, "Walks!"

That exclamation mark clearly reflected the caretaker's relief that I had finally reached a milestone that a child under normal conditions would have made more than a year before. Being stalled in my physical development was, in all likelihood, linked to the effects of traumas and malnutrition I suffered at Rēsekne Prison and Salaspils camp. Lagging behind on those milestones seems a small price to pay when I realize that I survived the illnesses, bullets, and bombs that ended the lives of so many others.

Alma Seķe-Mežaka.

Photo courtesy of Jānis Riekstiņš
Latvijas Bāreni, Mansards 2015

Walkway leading from the grounds where Golf Hotel
is thought to have stood in Hahnenklee, Germany.
May 2015 Photo by Marija Platace Futchs Fine

CHAPTER 9

Hahnenklee

The Big House

Hahnenklee

THERE IS NO way to know how we Rīga orphans went from the Goslar train station to Golf Hotel in Hahnenklee, several miles away. My guess is that we walked, something we did at various times in our journey from Swinemunde to Hahnenklee. The great advantage we now had was living in the safe haven that the mountains provided.

Germans took advantage of the cover the forest gave them by setting up a factory that produced rockets and grenades in Clausthal, just a few kilometers away from Hahnenklee. This industry replaced the silver mines that had been closed years earlier, thereby providing a much-needed source of livelihood for the population of fourteen thousand in several neighboring towns.[1]

The mountains provided another advantage—clean mountain air—that had made it suitable as a location for recreational activities such as golf and tennis since the 1930s. Because sportsmen and tourists stopped coming to Hahnenklee during the war, its hotels became a refuge for fleeing Russians and Polish refugees and for us Baltic orphans.

Three years before our arrival, when Germans were making their greatest military strides establishing the Third Reich, Hahnenklee became important both militarily and politically. Nazi builders constructed a wooden barracks in 1942 to accommodate about twenty Russian prisoners of war who were used for forestry work.

Hahnenklee was also a major location for its Lebensborn Association, where "racially pure" women gave birth to babies fathered by SS soldiers. The homes housed forty-five percent—or 3,600 of the 8,500 of the Lebensborn children born in Germany.[2] Nazis seized hotels and renamed them. Their names were Mother and Child, the Maternity House, the Recreation Home, and Sisters Recreation Home Hotel.

People involved in the Lebensborn Association and our group were not the only people converging on this small town. There were many displaced persons who fled along with us. Hahnenklee had a prewar size of 850 that tripled to 2,600 by the time we arrived.

Golf Hotel

Buildings were at a premium; they were repurposed many times such as our new home. Before Allied military units and our group of orphans moved into the Golf Hotel, several other groups had used it, including an American infantry regiment. After Germany's capitulation, which coincided with our arrival in Hahnenklee, the town came under the control of the British.

The British took over North Germany, while America, France, and Russia took over their assigned areas. Our town had a curfew that ran between 9:00 p.m. and 5:00 a.m., excluding the two Christmas Days, December 24–25, 1945. Fines—or even prison sentences—were threatened for any curfew violations.

Latvian orphan tracker Jānis Riekstiņš trained a spotlight on us in a newspaper article entitled "Bāreni Vācijā" (Orphans in Germany). He listed our names, where I appeared as Marija Platača. Of the ninety-two of us, sixty were boys and thirty-two were girls. Among them were fraternal twins with whom I became friends, Andris and Mirdza Levics/Leviņš, from Rīga.

Dr. Bergfelde described what happened in the first months after our arrival in the spring of 1945:[3]

> It was all chaos. At the beginning the American forces changed often, things promised by the first forces couldn't be delivered by the second because the third were on their way. As a result we barely made it through

the first six weeks—even the adults were barely moving, and 19 children had to be buried in a local cemetery. From 1945 our circumstances improved, soon children got all the necessities. Of course, we lacked fruit and vitamins, but we had enough protein.

Engineer A. Ludrikson of Germany wrote about those graves:[4]

In Hahnenklee, Harz Mountains, around 60 km south of Braunschweig . . . there was a lack of food, clothing and medicine. Many children died because of lack of care. I still saw their graves in the late 1960's. They might be flattened by now.

He was right in thinking that, because townspeople had flattened the graves. When I visited Hahnenklee in May 2015, there was no evidence of those tombs for orphans. There was no plaque mentioning them individually or as a group. People had possibly removed the earlier graves altogether or placed new graves on top of the ones for the orphans.

Despite those deaths, there were no epidemics in Hahnenklee, something caretakers feared. The focus then remained on food shortages, even among the general population. As Dr. Bergfelde went on to report,[5]

The supply of food, however, was a constant problem. Rations in the British zone had to be reduced to a near starvation level of 1,000 calories a day in March 1946, which limited workers' productive capacity, as they took time off from work to travel to the countryside for additional supplies. Rations did not exceed 1,500 calories a day until 1948–9, following a substantial increase in US financial aid and food exports to both the US and British zones. By comparison, food consumption in "austerity Britain" during the immediate post-war years was significantly higher, averaging 2,800 calories a day.

MARIJA PLATACE FUTCHS FINE

The same groups that had assisted the Latvian orphanages on their journeys through Germany—the Swedish Latvians in particular—stepped up to offer assistance to the Rīga Orphanage in Hahnenklee. They kept a constant spotlight on us by giving lists of what we needed to potential donors in an article, "Latvian News in Stockholm."[6]

Latvians in Koping, Sweden, raised 1,411 krones (US$174 in today's money) and sent 148.8 lb. of fat, 37.47 lb. of pig fat, 103.6 lb. of sugar, 22.5 lb. of coffee, 241.4 lb. of bread, 122 lb. of oat flakes, 4.4 lb. of cacao, 8.9 lb. of soap, among other things, in January 1949.

Other groups making appeals on our behalf directed donors to send supplies to A. Miller, the head of the orphanage committee, with the simple address Hahnenklee, Golf Hotel. Riekstiņš lauded these efforts, writing, "This human kindness has helped the little ones from Kapseļu Street to survive these hard days of hunger and lack. As well as self-sacrifice of their caretakers."

From 1945 to 1947, people inside and outside Germany knew our orphanage under three names: Kinder Haus (Children's House), Lettische Kinderheim (Latvian Children's Home), and the Rīga Waisenhaus in Deutschland (Rīga Orphanage in Germany). I called it the Big House.

It is hard to know the actual distance we actually covered, since we traveled by boat and train. But the land journey alone would have been more than six hundred miles from Swinemunde to Hahnenklee.

Hahnenklee held so much promise due to its location. It was a quiet, clean, and sunny shelter for us who had, up to this point, been scattered randomly by the storms of war. Looking out of the window of our home, we could see stately fir trees and blue mountaintops. Between two ponds—*Kranicher Teich and Kranicher Teich Kleiner*—there ran a narrow causeway. There was a grassy field next to our Kinder Haus.

Off in the distance was the famed Stave Church inspired by Norwegian wooden architecture. It was the one famous landmark every visitor to the town went to, according to townspeople I spoke with in Hahnenklee.

In the Kinder Haus, there were five to six children in a room, separated by age. My best friend, Mirdza, who, because she was two years older, probably slept in another room. Each of us had a bed, warm sheets, and white covers.

Staff made certain we celebrated birthdays and the Latvian Name Day with cookies and cocoa.[7] The staff thought the food was sufficient, if a bit dull, because at the high altitude where we were—2,624.6 feet above sea level—we had almost no fruit. Apples, pears, and plums were highly desired yet rare. Even though the food was bland, I had no problem taking it in. That is where I put on the pounds.

The Orphanage Record

When I entered Rīga Orphanage at sixteen months, I weighed 16.9 pounds, or 6 pounds lighter than the average American female of the same age, who weighed 22.5 pounds.[8] Even though my mother was breastfeeding me in the Latvian prison, her diet there was deficient. Conditions in the Salaspils nursery were no better. Regardless of the number of wet nurses there were at the Salaspils nursery, I did not receive sufficient nourishment. But after eating the dull diet in the Harz Hills for one year, I weighed 31.1 pounds, the exact weight of the average three-year-old American girl.

In terms of height, I was 28.32 inches long at sixteen months. The average length for American girls at that age was a full three inches longer, 31.4 inches. It would take me just two years to equal the average height of the American girl who was one year younger.

The one part of my record that had nothing to do with physical growth markers, one that surprised me, was an entry made by staff made on June 30, 1946. That was nearly two years after I entered the orphanage. It had to do with my religious affiliation.

When I entered the orphanage in 1944, there was a blank next to *krīstīts* (christened). Two years later, there was a handwritten abbreviation, *ev lut* (*Evaņģēliski luteriskā*, or Evangelical Lutheran), in that space.

I found it revealing that the category was not religion (*reliģija*), which would have allowed for children of all faiths. The entry *krīstīts*

MARIJA PLATACE FUTCHS FINE

reflected the Nazi expectation that its orphanages admitted only Christians, either Roman Catholic or Lutheran.

Jānis Riekstiņš thought that it was "unusual" for any clergyman to take the step of baptizing me. My guess is that one or more Lutheran ministers came to the orphanage to conduct church services for its staff and children on a regular basis. Hahnenklee was predominantly Lutheran.

Perhaps one of those Lutheran ministers asked the orphanage staff if any record showed that a child was not baptized. I was one such child. Since my record also showed that I was illegitimate, the orphanage staff might have assumed that was an additional reason for my not being baptized.

What the orphanage staff overlooked—intentionally or not— was that my record showed I was born in Andrupene, which is the one Roman Catholic region in Latvia.[9] Whatever the reason for that Lutheran pastor's actions, I was baptized twice, first as a Catholic in 1943, then as a Lutheran in 1946. That information would play a pivotal role at the time when staff made decisions as to where we were to be sent for overseas adoption.

First Memories

Under normal circumstances I should have been able to remember what happened when I was twenty-four or thirty months. But the traumas of the early years, which delayed standing and walking by as much as a year, probably also stalled my memory development.

My first memories were taste sensations and snapshots of scenes. One flavor that has come back hundreds of times over the years was the taste of rice pudding, so unique that I have never yet savored any pudding that has come anywhere near to what my taste memory suggests. It is probably one of those implicit memories frozen in my permanent body memory.

Visual memories include flashbacks to a picnic in a forest where there was a truck with food and children running around. There was the bleak scene of a schoolyard with a high wire fence around it, with children playing in the distance and the acute feeling of loneliness.

There was a scene of children screaming in some large hall we were in—some with feigned horror, others with gleeful excitement—when adults announced an older male figure dressed in some colorful costume was coming into the orphanage at Christmastime.

The first memory of an event that had a sequence of actions is what I call the Marble Incident. It was my first punishment, a very public one. It occurred during nap time, when we were supposed to be in our beds, resting. A group of us decided to play with some of these smooth tiny round playthings then.

Why did we decide to steal away during nap time? Were they kept for restricted use, so not everyone got to play with them during playtime? Were they a gift to the orphanage that caretakers kept under lock and key and one of us managed to purloin these exciting toys?

The marbles were something special. They were so different from the limited stock of toys at our disposal. In my recent research, I found Germany was the manufacturing center for marbles for centuries.[10] The golden age of marbles was in the 1920s and 1930s.

Several of us found our way to some secret place out of range of the housemothers, as we called them. As soon as we heard the footfall of one of them, my friends scattered, leaving me holding the marbles.

The housemother caught me red-handed. She told me punishment would be swift and very public. I was made to be the "example" who would stand at the head of the stairs on the landing while all the other children filed past me on their way to the party below. It could have been a Name Day party they were going to.

I stood there watching my guilty cohorts walk right past me in single file as they went down the stairs to the party. I remained there, crying the entire time, receiving public shaming followed by isolation. When a caretaker found me in tears, she asked what the problem was. After I explained my predicament, she thought it was totally unfair that I had shouldered this public humiliation. She said I should name the other children. I refused.

I might have been four or five years old then. When Mirdza's adoptive mother, Evelyn Hidy,[11] told me about how the two of us consoled each other in the orphanage, it was nice hearing that, even though I don't remember that occasion. It was probably Mirdza's shoulder I leaned on after the marble incident.

Repatriation or Immigration?

From 1947 onward, all of us became refugees—children as well as staff—and moved to new quarters. From recent pictures I saw of the outside of the building, it could have been a school. It certainly was not the wood-framed hotel we had been in earlier. The name of our new home was the Latvian DP Camp.

Concerns for our eventual fate were always on the minds of staff. Herberts Tērmanis, the man who replaced Dr. Bergfelde as the director of our DP center, was concerned that the Soviet Union, in its effort to repatriate us, would not allow us to know our culture.

He knew repatriation was a real possibility, since it was one of the agreements among leaders at the Potsdam Conference.[12] He wrote in the newspaper *Latviešu Ziņas* (*Latvian News*),[13]

> In the Harz hills, Hahnenklee town, almost a hundred Latvian orphans have found a home, yet Eastern tyrants won't stop reaching for their souls. The *boyars*[14] of the sickle can't accept that the destiny of these orphans is not in their hands.

Tērmanis was concerned that the great pains to which our Latvian caretakers went to inculcate in us the Latvian culture would be wiped out by foreign (Soviet) ideas on our return. He rued the fact that our fathers had fallen victims to fascism or that our mothers had died in concentration camps. He despaired over the fact that no Latvian publisher sent any books, that we had received just one cultural visit from the Latvian String Quartet.

Over the years, some extraordinarily good people had shepherded us through the journey out of Rīga, using every imaginable means of transport to move us from one dangerous location to another and always caring for our needs with scarce resources. Promising as our conditions were, there was an issue so difficult to resolve that it would keep us in Germany for two years. That was the issue of repatriation. While the Potsdam Agreement dictated that all DPs should return to their native homeland, it was by no means a fait accompli.

While authorities grappled over the issue of repatriation, which would ultimately decide my fate, other members of my family were struggling to adapt to a new world order. Helēna and Kazimirs were on the verge of returning to a Latvia that was under Soviet occupation for the second time in five years. Leonora was already becoming an adult as she and her siblings made it largely on their own. Meanwhile, my mother and father moved on their very different, individual paths.

LATVIEŠU BĀREŅI HANENKLEJĀ

Latviešu bāreņu mītne Hanenklejā.

Latvian orphanage, Hahnenklee, the Big House
Photo courtesy of Jānis Riekstiņš
Latvijas Bāreni, Mansards, 2015

Cemetery at Hahnenklee, 2015.
Nineteen children were buried there in 1945.
Photo by Marija Platace Futchs Fine

**Andris and Mirdza Leviņš (Drew and Marilyn Hidy)
Portland, Oregon in 1949**

**Latvian Displaced Persons Camp ca. 1948
Photos by Ross Hidy**

CHAPTER 10

Postwar Adjustments

Don't Run, I'm Your Mother

I N 1945, MY family transitioned from the wartime occupation of one government to the hostile domination of another regime in peacetime. Whether my family was taken by force to Germany or remained behind in Latvia, everyone faced the difficult demands of adjusting to a new world order.

Rather than making outward attacks on culture, religion, or freedom of expression, the Soviets began implementing a program of sovietization, a form of large-scale industrialization. Officials once again carried out massive deportations as they had done eight years earlier. They exiled persons who resisted collectivization or supported nationalist partisans (such as the Forest Brothers, who waged guerrilla tactics to bring back an independent Latvia).[1]

Broņislavs

After the Soviet victory on May 8, 1945,[2] my father resurfaced in Rīga. His former classmate, Oskars, who had recruited him for partisan work two years earlier, introduced Broņislavs to his friends in the capital city, standing ready to reward him for his partisan efforts.

Both he and brother Vitālijs became police recruits. My father learned to handle local police matters such as issuing identity cards called passports. That must have been an enormous adjustment, changing his livelihood from farming to desk work.

But since my father had less formal education than Vitālijs, he remained only six months in that job before moving to Dobele, forty-seven miles to the southwest of the capital. He began to earn income doing a variety of jobs, including house repair and carpentry work.

On her return to Latvia in 1945, Helēna did not know the fate of Solomeja or me, so she told my father guards had taken me from Solomeja in Salaspils concentration camp and that she never saw Solomeja after their boat journey out of Rīga Harbor.

Leonora said my father, Broņislavs; and his brother Vitālijs did not appear to have changed that much from their wartime experience. Although the brothers had suffered privations in the hostile environment of the Latvian swamps, they remained remarkably intact.

The whereabouts of two family members remained a mystery. No one knew the fate of Vladislavs, Helena's son from her first marriage, the man whom Nazis forced into conscription. Not surprisingly, Alberts, the family traitor, disappeared, never to be seen or heard from again.

Kazimirs and Helēna

Kazimirs and Helēna returned to a Soviet Latvia with its radically different political and economic order. Kazimirs lost his farm, which was collectivized, and resumed his trade as a tailor in Cēsis, fifty-five miles northeast of Rīga, at the foot of the Vidzeme Highlands, using a Latvian sewing machine. It was one of his two prized possessions, the other being an accordion, both of which he posed with for his "official" portrait.

Allied troops put former camp inmates such as Helēna onto trains to return to Latvia. She was weighed down with two suitcases full of expensive German dresses, which the liberating soldiers invited her to take to begin a new life in Latvia. The desperation and lawlessness that existed during the war were still evident. A young man, under the guise of asking to help her carry one of the suitcases onto the train, ran off with it.

After disembarking her train a few miles from Rusiški village, Helēna set out on foot for the last miles toward her village. When she entered the road nearest her home, Leonora was frightened by the sight of a bald woman with a dark complexion, holding a suitcase. Fearing the woman might be a Gypsy, Leonora ran inside her home.

She didn't recognize her own mother, who followed her into the house. Helēna was so physically changed that the sight of her repulsed Leonora. Helena tried calming her daughter by saying, "Don't run. I'm your mother." But Leonora was so overcome by the terrifying image of this strange, haggard woman that she actually passed out for a short time.

When she recovered, Leonora recalled seeing a woman so exhausted and forlorn that she thought she looked like a "baby bird fallen out of its nest." Leonora noticed another change in her mother. She did not understand Latgalian,[3] her mother tongue. Helēna had learned German to survive in her camp, and so she forgot most of her native tongue. For a while she couldn't understand anything Leonora said.

Helēna's rundown appearance was the result of working at her camp outside under the sun. Her loss of hair obviously came from stress and malnutrition. Over time, Helēna would tell Leonora about her personal travails starting from that night of March 13, 1944, on up through May 1945. But while her physical appearance may have changed, her personality remained unbroken.

Since Leonora still had contract work to fulfill at a neighbor's home nearly two miles away, she ran back to her home every evening to help her mother. They had to handle the condition of their home, which had fallen into disrepair during the war. Windows were smashed, and everything inside had to be fixed. Helēna and her children started to put the house back together.

To increase their resources, Helēna traded one of the dresses she carried in her suitcase for a cow. The war years had introduced a barter economy, which was still in effect on her return. She had little hope that she could hold on to their private farm, realizing that one year earlier, 1946, Stalin had started his war on kulaks, forcing them to turn over their private farms to the collective system known as kolkhoz.[4] If they didn't agree, they could be sent to Siberia, as many of them were in 1949.

Helēna met the Soviet regime's agrarian reforms head-on. She saw how officials took whatever measures were necessary to co-opt former kulaks to turn over their farms to the collective system. It was in this setting that Viktors Rukmanis once again reappeared as the menacing figure he had always been. He, who harassed my family as a Nazi collaborator, turned coat and began harassing Helēna on behalf of the Soviets.

He had become rich through his association with the Nazis, the only person in Andrupene who owned a small van and a two-story house after the war. Germans also elevated his political status to something approximating a governor.

He went over to Helēna's farm, pushed her against the wall, and ordered her to join the kolkhoz. Otherwise, he told her, the authorities would send her to Siberia for having made contact with Germans during her time in the concentration camps.

To assert that Helēna was making contact with the Germans in the concentration camps for political purposes was unimaginable. Just one year earlier, Rukmanis had played a role in arresting her husband for being a Soviet partisan, which led to his torture and death. Augusts had given his life as a Soviet partisan, and Helēna had nearly lost her life as a forced laborer in a Nazi concentration camp as a result of it.

But unfounded accusations and paranoia were the air that Soviets and Rukmanis breathed. The threats worked. My grandmother handed over almost everything the Platacis farm had to the nearby kolkhoz in Mākoņkalns (Cloud Mountain), which became the administrative unit of the Rēzekne municipality. The timing was quite unfortunate, as she had already bought a new horse, which she had to give away along with the cow, two sheep, several carts, and even a sled. She was left with only a baby calf.

Helēna worked at the kolkhoz, determined to be equal to the task, resolved to start a new life without Augusts. When the work was too exhausting, Leonora would sometimes go in her place to let her mother rest. Leonora remembers that she earned thirty-two kilograms (seventy pounds) of grain and some rubles that way.

Leonora wasn't involved in any matters related to the dissolution of the family farm, so she didn't remember if the size of their farm was cut down after the war or if the government demanded unusually high taxes or tolls. What she did remember was that they had to give a specified amount of butter every few weeks to the government. Sometimes that meant that when they didn't produce enough, they had to go to the market to buy it to give it to the Soviets.

Leonora

By the time Leonora resumed her education in 1945, she and her siblings were going to school in Mākoņkalns near Lake Rāznas, the largest lake in Latvia. She was embarrassed about having to wear old, worn clothes, but no one made fun of her because she was a top student at her school.

Leonora finished seven grades, continuing to make excellent marks in every subject. She went to Rīga, where she spoke Russian to hide the fact that she was from Latgale. She felt that urbanites looked down on Latgalians as stupid and poor.

Leonora wanted to work in the medical field. She applied to nursing school. As one of her first assignments, she went to the morgue to study the cadaver of a murdered criminal. The sight of a man with his stomach torn apart was so sickening that she gave up thinking of entering the medical profession.

Her sights turned to tailoring. Her mother had taught her those skills, which she had put to use at so young an age, knitting those "trousers" for me in one instance. She took tailoring courses for three years and then worked for a clothing company.

She also did freelance work to make clothes for friends and family using a sewing machine. She charged a few rubles for each piece. The cost of a machine that could do special seams was 1,200 rubles (US$17).

Leonora looked back on those times and observed that though the family lost everything because of the war, they were resilient. Everything was beginning to look up. Broņislavs was building his new house in Dobele while Vitālijs was doing the same elsewhere.

Brother Vitālijs secured a flat for her, where she lived with a teacher for two years. Those were Soviet times, so the government provided her flat. A Jewish family swapped their home for Leonora's flat. Later on, sister Malvīna moved in with her, followed by Helēna, who worked as a cleaning lady.

Leonora married twice in the two decades following the war. The first marriage was to Gunārs Ķieģelis, with whom she had a son, Aivars, born in 1954. The second marriage was to Indulis Okuško, with whom she had a son, Valdis, born in 1962.

The way Leonora met Gunārs was evidence of her charm and confidence. When a girlfriend of hers had "picked off" the boyfriend Leonora had, that emboldened her to take matters into her own hands.

She made a bet with another girlfriend that she would go to a dance hall and marry the first gentleman to come up to ask her to dance. On that night in February 1954, a handsome man in uniform came up to her and asked for a dance. A few months later, in May, they were married in St. John's Church.

She liked it that Gunārs was well built and tall. But she didn't like it that he smoked. Tried as he did to kick the habit, he couldn't. Gunārs died eight years into his marriage. He had contracted gangrene in both legs frozen while serving in the army up north.

Leonora—as with most Latvians—loved to sing. She participated in the Song and Dance Festival in 1949. The government had its list of accepted songs, as censorship was very strict. However, when thousands of people were on the stage, it was hard to control what they sang, so Latvians did chant revolutionary anthems. That festival was in large part an activist event, aimed at exciting Latvians to see their country become, once again, independent.

Leonora had traveled nearly twenty-two miles in a truck to the festival, which she and her friends could only use one way to participate with her choir. They had to walk back, sleeping overnight in the woods. To keep up their spirits, Leonora and her friends sang her favorite

Latgalian folksong, *Ziedi, ziedi rudzu vārpa* ("Bloom, Bloom, Oh Rye Ear"):

> *Bloom, bloom, oh rye ear*
> *With nine branches*
> *My brothers are building a barn*
> *With nine compartments*
> *Make what you make, my brothers*
> *But build me a room*
> *With three doors*
> *Sun rises through one*
> *And sets through another*
> *I walk through the third*
> *Myrrh wreath on my head*

Solomeja

While Helēna, Leonora, and Kazimirs struggled to rebuild their lives after repatriating to Soviet Latvia, my mother remained in Germany along with sixty thousand other survivors of the German concentration camps.

They represented a tiny fraction of the total number of displaced persons, or twelve million. DP camps were in Germany, Austria, Italy, and other countries. One camp was even set up in North America, in Guanajuato, Mexico.[5] The lives of millions of refugees went on for the better part of a decade in these holding centers.

My mother and I were among the 83,111 Baltics in British DP camps. Estonians were the smallest Baltic group, with 13,059, or fifteen percent. Lithuanians numbered 23,555, or twenty-three percent. The Latvians, the largest group, numbered 45,497, representing nearly fifty-seven percent of the overall total.[6]

Allied forces placed us into improvised shelters that ran the gamut, from former barracks, to summer camps for children, airports, hotels, castles, hospitals, private homes, and even partly destroyed structures. There were thousands of facilities, which Allies tried to name assembly centers. They wanted to avoid the hated term of *camps* associated with the despised concentration camps from which many of the survivors had come and were now refugees. But in the end, the term *camp* stuck.

Rendsburg DP Camp

My mother chose to stay in a German DP camp for the next eighteen months, reasons for which I can only form tentative explanations. Those reasons did not even come up in the standard exit interrogations she had with the Soviets at the time she decided to return to Latvia.

Health professionals who observed the behavior of women who—like my mother—lost a child in concentration camps, made some observations about their behavior and how they overcame their loss. Some case workers found that these women exhibited defeminization, a decline in the maternal instinct and an unconcern for their bodies. One UNRRA worker wrote,[7]

> Many "let themselves go" physically and emotionally . . .
> It seemed as if the majority of women lost all interest in
> life . . . These conditions were unbearable for all of us.
> It was necessary to shake women out of their lethargy
> . . . we attempted, as much as possible, to take care of
> our appearances, and through our example to show that
> even under these living conditions, one should not lose
> their bearings.

Mothers who experienced the abrupt loss of a child, however, overcame the decline in their maternal instinct once they were freed from a concentration camp and entered a DP camp. The most influential factor that improved the recovery of a childless mother was her age. The younger she was, the greater chance she had of regaining her sense of self.

Medical professionals who worked with freed female prisoners in Bergen-Belsen discovered how their age profoundly affected their post camp experience. Sex played a key "role in that survival." One case worker said, "Sex may have preoccupied the young but older survivors had a single thought—to find out the fate of relatives."[8]

That worker described how that focus on sex helped younger female Belsen inmates, most of them Jewish, regain their physical and mental health, stating that,

> most therapy at Belsen was done by the inmates themselves. It took three principal forms, a rediscovery of the body, a reconnection with families and a reassertion of Jewishness. . . . The young women . . . wanted to "live" rather than to "think" . . . women remembered the joy they felt as their breasts returned and they began to menstruate again. . . . After liberation there was sex going on in the camp—in the forest area. Sometimes people found their mates there, and they came home and got married. They were young people, men and women of all ages thrown together.

If Solomeja had remained at Bergen-Belsen when it was liberated, she quite possibly would have joined in on the same activities as the other women in the camp did. But since she was healthy enough to be taken out in the first group of released prisoners, she had to wait to carry out her plan at the camp the British eventually took her to.

At the time the British released former inmates from Belsen, Solomeja made it clear to the British she had no desire to return to Latvia. That meant only one thing: she would report to a DP camp to decide what her next steps would be.

Her resolve was clear on one point. She would not return to my father, for whom she had been an unwilling hostage. She would find a new life with a German and stay there. She arrived at this decision long before liberation came.

Her mental journey possibly started at Salaspils camp when she befriended a guard in hopes that he would help her to reclaim me. Or—if she did become pregnant as Helēna suspected—that might have been a way to regain her own mental and emotional strength by having a replacement baby.

As she moved from camp to camp, she might have imagined how she would leave the past behind and begin life anew with someone else. So once liberation came, Solomeja might have had the idea of staying in Germany, where she could start a new family. If that is how she felt, her assignment to Rendsburg was propitious. She had a paying job and easy access to a nearby town, where she could use her earned money to buy clothes and meet her German who would marry her, father her child, and with whom she would remain.

So where my mother's age possibly motivated her to remain in Germany to start a new family there, age worked in a very different way with regard to Kazimirs and Helēna. They were considerably older than Solomeja, Helēna by thirty years, Kazimirs by twenty years. Both of them had children waiting for them back in Latvia, and in my great uncle's case, he also had a wife waiting for him.

They were among the older camp survivors for whom there was a single thought—to find out the fate of relatives having family to return. It gave them the impetus to reconnect with their loved ones back home.

My mother arrived at Rendsburg, located in the region of Schleswig-Holstein, one of the hundreds of refugee camps maintained by the British. The camps' inhabitants—Latvians, Lithuanians, and Poles—were self-organized and self-managed. That allowed leaders from the various ethnic communities to emerge. Latvians published their own newspapers and periodicals and staffed their own medical facilities and schools. They carried on their cultural life through art, crafts, literature, and music. Many hoped that within months they would return home, based on their belief that Allies would respect the Atlantic Charter by driving out the Soviets from Latvia.[9]

The Rendsburg camp was a relatively small one, housing just several hundred persons. It had a parade ground with rectangular and rounded buildings. Latvians worked in the administrative offices of the Rendsburg camp. There was a hospital where a doctor and nurse were always on site. The British paid for medical treatments of the camp's residents.

Latvians at the camp established a school where teenagers Ruta Praulina, Rita Drone, and Maija Stumbris were students. Lauris found Ruta through his search of persons who had been at Rendsburg and thought she might have met my mother there.

I interviewed all three ladies at Ruta's home in Minneapolis in March 2015.[10] Though they didn't know my mother, they gave enough details so that I came away with a snapshot of the camp setting. All were teenagers during their time at the Rendsburg camp.

The diet in the camp included cornbread, green beans, and peas. Lemons were highly prized. They also had, to use their words, ersatz coffee. They used hotplates that spawned all kinds of creative cooking ideas, such as putting raisins in their soup.

Life in the DP camp was comfortable. Some even found it fun, as they had none of the worries that burdened their parents who worried about the country they left behind and the uncertainties of what lay ahead.

Gates were open at all times. One could actually look into Rendsburg from inside the camp. The town had shops where one could buy clothing and movie houses where residents could watch German movies, including comedies.

Baltic refugees also stayed in the nearby assembly centers at Kiel (twenty-three miles) and Fockbek (fewer than four miles), which had a British army barracks. My mother told the NKVD interrogator her work assignment at the DP camp was in the army mail. Rita suggested that might have been where my mother lived and worked from May 1945 to December 1946. That would explain why they would not have known her.

Germans were not invited into the camp, but one could meet them in the town. Ruta, Rita, and Maija said there was an easy flow in and out of the camp, so Solomeja probably had no difficulty using her earnings to buy clothing, dress up, and go to places where she could meet her German.

She succeeded in the first part of that plan. On November 3, 1946, Solomeja gave birth to a baby boy. But then she had a problem. Her German, for whatever reason, didn't go along with her plan. As I try to divine the reasons why he did not keep her there with him, a number of scenarios come to mind.

Perhaps she found out he was married, or he turned her away for another reason. Maybe his family didn't accept her, or he didn't want to be a father. It could have been a love match, but while he might have wanted to go with her, he knew he wouldn't gain entry into Soviet Latvia as a German. He might have even died in an untimely accident.

She knew she was alone and that there was no way she could survive in Germany. She didn't know the language and had no meaningful job skills. So, on December 20, 1946, she approached the Soviet officials who were allowed to enter Rendsburg DP camp to repatriate Soviet citizens back to Latvia. Soviets took the two of them—Solomeja and her baby—to the Wolow filtration camp in Poland for the standard exit interrogation for all Soviet citizens leaving Germany.

Solomeja knew that returning to Latvia with a child fathered by a German was not going to be welcomed in a village with very traditional ideas about family. She had no choice but to come up with a plausible story so she could sail against the tide of public opinion.

As I reviewed the movements of my mother, I became fixated on maps to see how far we were from each other in the various German cities we lived in. When my mother was held at Stutthof concentration camp and I was in a school building in Swinemunde, there was a distance of two hundred fifty-seven miles between us.

When Germans shifted her to Neuengamme concentration camp and I remained at Swinemunde, we came thirty-nine miles closer (two hundred-eighteen miles). But for the months she was at Bergen-Belsen and I was at Hahnenklee's Golf Hotel, we were the closest we would ever be: eighty-nine miles. The distance between us increased when we were both in DP camps. While she was at Rendsburg for those eighteen months beginning in April 1945 and I was in Hahnenklee, two hundred-fourteen miles separated us.

While my mother was on her way back to Latvia in December 1946, a highly charged debate started between Soviets and the British over the fate of all of us orphans. It was a political issue further complicated by inadequate or nonexistent records as to who our parents were.

My father on the phone at the police station, Rīga, 1945
Photo from Leonora Platace's family album

The building in Rīga where my father had a flat in 1945,
as it appeared in August 2015
Photo by Marija Platace Futchs Fine

CHAPTER 11

The Divorce

My Doors Are Closed to You

Interrogation

MOST REPATRIATED CITIZENS went through interrogation with the NKVD,[1] including my mother. Her NKVD files were kept in secret case archives until September 6, 1957. The first session took place in Poland in 1946; two others took place in Latvia in (probably) 1947 and 1949.

There were misstatements or answers that didn't fit a particular question, but it is hard to tell if the mistakes were deliberate or the result of incompetence. For example, she gave two answers for the number of school grades she completed. In one interview she said three grades; in another, it was six.

One interrogator wrote a note that she planned to repatriate to Lithuania and Rīga. The same person wrote the puzzling comment that my mother was taking care of a daughter, Valentīna Platač, born November 3, 1946. But it was a boy, whom she named Andris.

Useful pieces of information included the fact that she had two jobs at the Rendsburg DP camp. She worked at a farm "doing different duties," and for the army mail number 14509, where she was content with the salary, and had no debts. A selected sampling of the interrogator's questions and her answers follow:

Q: Are you a member of the communist party or other organization?

A: Not a member

Q: Platach, please tell us how you ended up in the camp.

A: I got there 13th of March 1944, on the grounds of disloyalty and for supporting the partisans. My husband was also a partisan. The police took me and my daughter, aged 1 year 2 months, drove us to Rēzekne Prison, then Salaspils camp, where we stayed till 12 of August 1944. Then I was taken to German camp Stutthof.

Q: Were you arrested, detained, fined, or commit any other criminal activity on the German side?

A: No

Q: Did you receive letters from home?

A: No

Q: Did you serve in the army, hospital, construction, etc.?

A: Freed by the English. Came to the camp with army forces.

Q: Anything to add?

A: Nothing to add. The protocol correctly represents my words. I have read it and signed it.

I wondered how villagers reacted to her return. Ben Shephard wrote about the reception that liberated inmates from Bergen-Belsen and other camps experienced, that they would "face subtle discrimination for the rest of their lives."[2]

That would not be the only reason my mother met with an unwelcome reception. She arrived carrying her illegitimate baby. Though still married to my father, she defied all the conventions of traditional village life by proclaiming her German, whom she called her husband, would come to join her and their newborn.

While a few villagers may have been sympathetic toward my mother, she became the object of ridicule and scorn for most. I have wondered if the negative attitude of villagers, not to mention the unfavorable regard among members of my father's family, was the reason why no pictures of her have surfaced. Lauris sought those pictures but reported that family or acquaintances had lost or destroyed her pictures. He agreed that "this relentless destruction of her photos is quite mysterious."

Helēna disliked the way my mother—with no hint of embarrassment—announced that her German would be joining her in several months. Solomeja's act of defiance dismayed her mother-in-law, who had not approved of Broņislavs's choice to marry Solomeja in the first place. She and Augusts had hoped their firstborn would marry another girl.

Solomeja told Helēna that the reason she returned was because she missed her. That may have been the reason after the fact, not the real one, which was that her plans to stay in Germany fell through. Her story about her German has never added up. Solomeja never gave the name of her German, where he came from, or any other details about him.

Helēna's disappointment with her daughter-in-law went to the very heart of the moral dilemma many people faced in the war. Some met that test with the strength of their unbending character, but others less equipped to handle the assault on their morals ended up compromising their values.

Shephard addressed that very point when he talked about the hard choices confronting liberated inmates. As they went from the mad world of war to the sane world of peacetime, he observed that prisoners who had "found it difficult to function in a world without morality and humanity, now found it difficult to relate to ordinary people, to have normal feelings."[3]

Did the choices my mother made in the concentration camps give her anguish? Did turning her back on my father disturb her? I think they did. But regardless of what she did, I don't judge her. She is my mother, who was crushed by the events around her.

And there was a happy ending to the standoff between Solomeja and Helēna. Helēna made peace with her in the end. She was the one who initiated the reconciliation.

Divorce

Broņislavs came from Dobele to Andrupene to meet my mother. They stayed in separate houses and had their last conversation at the home of my father's cousin, Rozālija.

It was a tense standoff, during which I am certain my father saw a changed woman. The last time he saw his Solomeja, she was a young mother holding tightly onto their firstborn, looking at him with frightened eyes as he quickly gathered his personal items before bounding out of our home for Lubāna swamp with his brother and fellow partisans.

Now he faced a defiant Solomeja, who blamed him for everything that had happened to her. He must have felt as much guilt as helplessness in the situation. He wanted to reunite with her, but my mother rebuked him, saying, "My man is coming this autumn. My doors are closed to you." Within months, they were divorced, Soviet style. It was a matter-of-fact process involving signing a few papers.

I thought how the war not only destroyed their marriage but also continued to reach down into the lives of two of their children in their second marriages. The firstborn from my father's second marriage drank himself to death before he reached the age of forty, and my mother's only son died a senseless death at the age of forty-seven at the hands of his wife's lover.

It brought to mind Agate Nesaule's WWII refugee experiences, when she observed that "family relationships and historical events intersected to inflict wounds . . . the way that wartime horrors affect even those in the next generation who never went to war."[4]

My Mother, Post Divorce

Solomeja moved back in with her mother, who despised her daughter's German baby. While living in Valusja she joined the kolkhoz in Mākoņkalns, where she milked cows for the rest of her life. Her German never came.

I talked with her supervisor, Monika Gribuste, in 2014. She knew Solomeja by her maiden name, Danovksa, since she was divorced from

Broņislavs by then. Monika had no knowledge of my mother before the war. She only knew her as a hardworking individual who never missed a day of work.

Leonora never saw my mother's baby boy, but Helēna did. She told her he had allergic reactions to most everything he ate. He had a constant skin rash and a poor appetite. He died at eighteen months.

On the few occasions Leonora saw my mother, Solomeja made comments that were poignant, spiteful, or self-pitying. Once she said to Leonora, "I hope your life will be happier than mine has been." Another time she said, "I have nowhere to go. I am stuck in this farm shit." But the words that must have cut Leonora to the quick were when Solomeja, grasping onto Leonora's shoulders, said, "Dear Leonora, I wish I had not met your brother."

Sometime after that, she met and married Andrejs Kairišs, a man who was fifteen years her senior. Whenever someone brought up his name in my 2014 visit to Latvia, they mentioned the age difference between my mother and her second husband. The fact that they had a May to December marriage caused me to speculate.

Was my mother looking for a father figure, someone who would protect her after all her travails in the war? In 1963 Solomeja and Andrejs welcomed a son, Andris. Three years later, 1966, Solomeja's husband died. Solomeja was once again a single parent, raising Andris.

My Father's Life, Post Divorce

The son from his second marriage, Andris, told me our father never held a grudge against Solomeja, nor did he ever badmouth her. He must have felt enormous guilt over leaving the two of us to an uncertain fate. But at that time, he believed Germans would not take women and children.

He returned to Dobele, saddened at losing his family but ready to find a wife with whom to start a new family in the house and barn he built. He continued his work as a policeman until he was forty-five, the mandatory retirement age, and performed odd jobs as a repairman, using his masterful carpentry skills.

When he went to a home in a nearby village to fix a roof, he met Antonija Orbitāne, whom he married in both a church and civil ceremony in 1951. In 1954, he and his wife, Antonija, welcomed the birth of their first son, Jānis. The following year, 1955, a second son, Andris, was born.

My Father's Search

It seems Broņislavs decided to search for me after he remarried. Perhaps he thought that if he couldn't get his wife back, he would at least bring back his daughter into his new family. Leonora told me about the first approach he used, going to Rīga Orphanage. Lauris came across the second approach, my father's use of newspaper ads. And the ITS surprised me by revealing his third method, an appeal he made to the Russian Red Cross.

Each of these methods broke down due to problems involving information, the lack of it and poor coordination among data files. There was no coordination between the groups, which, had they been able to piece together the information each of them had, there might have been a successful outcome.

Leonora thinks that my father went to Rīga Orphanage in 1953, just two years shy of my becoming a US citizen. The orphanage, under Soviet management, steered my father in the wrong direction. Soviet authorities—for whatever reason—did not provide a list they had with my name on it with the heading "Placed for adoption overseas."

What the staff did instead was inexplicable. They told him I was living at a home with a couple on Kirova Street and gave him the address. Broņislavs went to the home and announced himself to a young girl who looked to be about my age. He said, "I'm your father!" She glared back and retorted, "You're not my father!" Her parents backed her up on that fact. My father broke down in tears.

I have no idea what the process the Soviet Union in the 1950s was for claiming missing children in the war. There had to be more to the story than what Leonora could remember. It's strange that the orphanage would take my father at his word and, without asking him to file some papers, allowed him to go alone to a home to claim his daughter.

It also wasn't clear what the girl's legal status was. Was she a foster child? Or was she already formally adopted? Regardless of how many stages were involved in my father's search at the orphanage, the Soviets either intentionally misled him or used inaccurate information.

In 1957, my father's next approach was advertising through two Latvian newspapers published by Russia in East Berlin. They aided Latvian families to bring out-of-country Latvians home. The monthly publications were *Par atgriešanos Dzimtenē* (*About Returning Home*)[5] and *Dzimtenes Balss* (*Homeland Voice*).[6]

Broņislavs placed the first of three ads, which appeared in the March, June, and July issues of *Par atgriešanos Dzimtenē*, in a section entitled "Your relatives back home are looking and waiting for you." People who read the ads were living in Eastern Europe, even though hundreds of us orphans were no longer in Germany, East or West. The Soviets knew that, but the Latvians reading the paper didn't know that.

The ad he placed in March 1957, gave the obligatory nod to the current propaganda by referring to the Nazis who kidnapped me as "fascists."

Fascists took Marija, daughter of Broņislavs, born 30th of May 1943 and put her in Rēzekne prison alongside her mother in 13th of March 1944, then she was sent to Hahnenklee, Germany in 1948 (British occupied zone). Her father Broņislavs Platacis is looking for her. His address: Latvian SSR, Dobele, Uzvaras street 20.

In the name of all the relatives and myself I turn to the Committee with a plea to help me find my child. I ask for the Committee's care to return my child to me as soon as possible. All relatives are still alive, all are working, and our only wish is to see Marija in our midst.

The last two ads appeared in 1959 in the newspaper *Dzimtenes Balss*. Both gave the incorrect information that I was in the Majori Republican Orphanage.

> *Broņislavs Platacis is again looking for his daughter Marija Platace, born 1943, who, along with 150 other children, was taken by Germans from Majori Republican orphanage in 1944 and taken to Germany*
>
> *(Their address was Glosar, Obergarz, Hannenklee, Lettische Kinderheim).*
> *His address: Latvian SSR, Dobele, Uzvaras street 20, flat 1.*

Apart from the incorrect information was that these ads made no reference to my imprisonment at Salaspils concentration camp. My mother and Helēna told him that important fact, but for some reason, he never used it.

The third approach my father used was making a formal inquiry at the Russian Red Cross in 1959, which is something I chanced upon. After the ITS sent eight pages detailing my mother's time in two concentration camps, a staff member wrote to say they might have files on me. Claudia Emde of the Tracing and Fate Clarification Department wrote,[7]

> On completion of your late mother's file we found out that there might be information about yourself in our archives, too. For verification purposes we kindly ask you to give us your father's personal data. Did you come to the USA together with your mother? If you did not, please let us know when you got in contact with your mother and what happened to your father.

Those questions puzzled me. Did I come to the USA with my mother? Did I have contact with her? Surely they had someone else in mind. But I gave them the information. Who knows? I might find out something interesting. And I did.

Within a week I received a three-page cover letter giving an outline of my father's search for me, which started about the same time when he placed his last newspaper ads, in 1959. There were dozens of pages containing correspondence between Red Cross agencies from five nations.

In its cover letter, the ITS agent stated, "Your natural parents were searching for you; your father indicated in his inquiry that you possibly died in 1944." As I skimmed through the pages, I was amazed to find multiple spellings for both given and family names. *Marija* appeared once; *Maria* came up most often. Some persons used my patronymic name, Maria Bronislava or Maria Bronislavna, my patronymic names since it was during Soviet times. But it was my surname that ran the gamut. There were eight spellings, among them Platcts, Platasch, and Platotsch.

It was the "Clearance Form for an Unaccompanied Child," drafted by the International Relief Organization (IRO), that proved to be the most curious. It recommended "that the child be considered for resettlement in accordance with IRO Provisional Order No. 75," which included "resettlement abroad with a view to adoption in a few years, in case the mother could not be found."

What widened my eyes in amazement was seeing the name of the person who witnessed my record, Dr. Veronika Bergfelds. The Clearance Form identified her as "former Leader and Chief-Doctor, now living in DP camp, Clausthal-Zellerfelda."

She signed off on the form. Fourteen years later, she reported to me via her niece that I was legitimate, my mother died in childbirth, and my father was fighting against the communists. The years had, indeed, clouded her memory. She had mixed me up with another child. The report read,

> The child has been admitted to the State Children's Home on 2.9.44 (September 2, 1944) because her mother **went** [emphasis mine] to Germany in August 1944. Nothing is known on the mother and the circumstances in which she left her child behind . . . [it is not known] whether the child was legitimate or if there were any relatives. Tracing of the mother remained without success.

By saying that that my mother "left her child behind," and that there was a question about my legitimacy, showed how Germans had effectively erased the names of my parents. And Dr. Bergfelds signed off on it, only to say to me through her niece nearly fourteen years later that I was legitimate.

If British officials had been in possession of my mother's Stutthof file, they could have cross-referenced it with my orphanage record. They would have found a match.

The Stutthof file gave the names of both of my parents, showed my mother had one child, and indicated that she was hostage for the husband, Broņislavs. My Rīga orphanage had on record that I came from Salaspils camp—known to hold relatives of Soviet partisans—as well as my date of birth, Andrupene origins, and that my mother went to Germany.

All the British needed to do was connect these two files, but they didn't have access to the Stutthof record. The Allies only found some German camp records to help IRO officials to find missing relatives, but not the one for my mother. So they had to proceed with the Clearance Form.

In 1961, my father learned what happened to me. A letter addressed to Lavina Johnson, the director of the National Enquiry Bureau, on December 11, 1961, reported,

> For your confidential information we would like to add that this child has been adopted, however, the appropriate agency does not wish to release any information regarding her whereabouts.

So my father learned I was adopted and living somewhere in the world. He would never know who adopted me or in what country. The efforts my father made to find me gave me several heart-stopping moments. But all his efforts came too late. As I pored over these newspaper ads and Red Cross letters, tears welled up from inside me. Tears were the one tangible, physical connection I had to the man whose blood ran through me. It's the closest I came to actually feeling him.

**Christening of Aivars, firstborn child
of Leonora and Gunārs, 1955
My father is at the far right. His wife,
Antonija, is next to Gunārs.**

My father with his first son, Jānis, ca. 1959

Photos from Leonora Platace's family album

The house and barn my father built, Dobele, 2014
Photos by Marija Platace Futchs Fine

Left: Front page of newspaper *Dzimtenes Balss*, September 1959
Right: The ad my father placed on page 4

The wedding of Leonora and Gunārs, 1954
My father and his second wife, Antonija, are in
the third row, the last two on the far right.

The wedding of Leonora and Jānis, 2007
Photo from Leonora Platace's family album

CHAPTER 12

Immigrants

Answer for Anne

Stateless People

A S MY PARENTS were in the process of dissolving their marriage, my fate in the Hahnenklee orphanage was still in flux, which was just as true for the eleven to twenty million other refugees in 1945. We were the largest number of stateless people in the history of the planet, searching for a safe harbor.[1]

The United Nations Relief and Rehabilitation Administration (UNRRA) housed and fed six million of us in the DP camps with varying degrees of success. A fraction, four percent, of those displaced persons (DPs) were the two hundred forty thousand Latvians who migrated to DP camps in Germany, Austria, and other countries in 1946.[2] In Germany alone, one hundred seventy-one thousand Balts stayed in one of the camps run by the Allies; forty-five percent lived in the British Zone, fifty-two percent in the USA Zone, and two and half percent in the French Zone.

The best guesstimate for the number of unaccompanied children in the DP camps was twenty thousand.[3] Based on 1943 census data, those of us who were fifteen years or younger represented just under eighteen percent of the total Latvian exile community.[4] The several hundred of us from Rīga and Majori orphanages were an even smaller part of the "hard-core" contingent of refugee children who remained in Germany for years. The UNRRA viewed the camps that housed unaccompanied children as[5] self-declared laboratories, where humanitarian workers debated new ideas about child development and human nature through their observation of individuals displaced by war and racial persecution.

Unaccompanied children became the symbols of both wartime dislocation and postwar renewal. But the campaign to restore us was far from a unified one. Historian Zahra described the two competing views on our fate:

> It openly pitted the collectivist visions of nationalist, Zionist, and socialist child welfare experts against the psychoanalytic and familialist theories of British and American psychoanalysts and humanitarian workers.

> Activism around displaced and refugee children ultimately became a forum for more fundamental debates about human psychology and development; the nature of trauma, the emotional consequences of separating children from parents, and the value of familial versus collective education.

While there were forces pulling to return us to Latvia, there were equally strong forces pulling us toward overseas adoption. Zahra described the conflict as "the rise of humanitarian activism around children."

Whether to return or relocate refugees became the focus of international conventions that tackled the issue head-on. The first guiding principles came from the Potsdam Protocol of 1945. A more expanded version—the Universal Declaration of Rights—came three years later in 1948.[6]

Both agreements addressed the issue of repatriation. But where the Potsdam Protocol dictated the return of DPs to their homeland, the Declaration of Rights allowed for a choice in the matter.

Repatriation: The Soviet View

Soviets embraced the Potsdam Agreement. They regarded all refugees from their captured lands were Soviet citizens who should return. That included all the "stolen children" Germans had kidnapped.

Soviets had a clear self-interest in supporting repatriation, as it was key to their reconstruction. Zahra pointed out that their repatriation campaign was also linked to the legitimacy of their new postwar government. Returning their "citizens" played a central role in the reconstruction in their ruined economies.

They depended on repatriates to replace those who had died on the battlefield, who could start the physical and intellectual work of reconstruction. The refusal of displaced persons to return home represented nothing less than an act of treason to newly established Communist governments in the East.

The Soviets had their allies in their efforts to repatriate us, among them the international humanitarian workers, even including the Hahnenklee orphanage staff. Aid workers argued in favor of repatriation, influenced by the studies of child psychologists Ann Freud, Dorothy Burlingham, and Therese Brosse.

UNRRA and IRO social workers spoke of acting in children's "best interests," which to them meant reuniting them with their biological families, especially mothers and children. They wanted to rebuild shattered families. They argued that the "trauma" of war for children was not the result of violence and hunger, but instead the trauma of separation from their mothers.

Repatriation was not without its obstacles. It required verifying the identity of children, a nearly impossible task, since Nazis had stolen thousands of our birth records. There were thousands of us who were undocumented.

But Soviets pressed on in their campaign to repatriate families and undocumented children who were born in countries they occupied. They published our names that the Latvian DP camp gave them in the newspaper *Cīņa (The Fight)*, on November 30, 1947, that neither Broņislavs nor Solomeja saw.

Latvian organizations welcomed the publication, willing to overlook the dreaded political reality Latvian orphans would experience in a Soviet Latvia. They wanted to return as many Latvian children as they could as part of the effort to rebuild its decimated population.

Latvia had lost even more of its people than either Estonia or Lithuania. Due to killings, emigration, and deportations, guesstimates were that Latvia lost approximately thirty percent of its prewar population during WWII. This compared to the twenty percent loss of Estonia's population and fifteen percent loss of Lithuania's population.[7]

Our orphanage staff became strong advocates for returning us to Latvia from the Latvian DP camp. They wrote letters to the Latvian community, which a variety of publications carried. Two caretakers sent a letter to the Soviet Military Mission of Repatriation of Soviet Citizens in the English Zone in West Germany:[8]

> We, Soviet citizens Jeļena Meinerte and Emma Lapiņa, are currently residing in the British Zone of West Germany, Soviet citizen repatriation point. Meinerte has worked in Rīga Orphanage since 1st of May 1944, Lapiņa since October 7, 1945. It housed orphans and children whose parents were arrested by Germans. While living in the repatriation point, we wrote a letter to Soviet generals about this orphanage in the English zone. After reading the article *'I testify and accuse'* by our compatriot Zelma Vītiņa, published in 1947, a publication of newspaper *Trud*, we ask the Soviet Military mission of repatriation to further spread this message.

The British developed a strong opposition to the Soviets. They were among the first Allied officials who rejected the tenets of the Potsdam Protocol on repatriation. Where refugee families were concerned, they allowed Soviet liaison officers to visit refugee camps in its zone to make their appeals to families to return to Latvia. Officials of the Bolshevik occupation used different propaganda brochures and appeals, but their success was minimal. Only 1,079 Latvian civilians and 3,600 former Latvian soldiers returned.[9]

Where British officers allowed refugee families the choice of accepting or rejecting Soviet appeals to return to Communist countries, they drew the line at unaccompanied children. They were galvanized by Article 15 of the 1948 Universal Declaration of Rights that cited the "right to a nationality."

The Declaration allowed a choice, invoking the principle that "no one shall be arbitrarily deprived of his nationality nor denied the right to change his nationality." In view of the British, repatriation was just one—unacceptable—way to "rehabilitate" displaced children. Transnational adoption was the other—preferred—means to restore them.

While international agencies, Latvian groups, UNRRA's successor, the IRO, lined up on the side to argue for repatriation, officials in the British Zone began to explore transnational adoption in the United States, Canada, Australia, and South America.

Complicating matters were officials in London and Washington who began equivocating on the issue of repatriation. Washington issued strong anti-Soviet statements, only to back off from them. Austrian journalist Gitta Sereny, a child welfare officer with the UNRRAs working in the US zone of Germany, found this kind of vacillation[10]

> disturbing when we learned late that summer of 1946 that Washington was considering issuing a fanatically anti-Soviet order (and seeking agreement to it in Britain) to resettle all children of Russian origin—including those from the contested Ukrainian and Baltic border regions—in the U.S., Australia, and Canada, instead of returning them to their homes and a life under the Soviets.

> Continual changes in the rulings we received over the months were confusing and disturbing, and we were finally convinced that no one in authority understood

either the political complexities or the human conflicts that surrounded us and our charges.

In the midst of this seesaw battle over whether to repatriate us or carry on with transatlantic adoptions, the IRO set up child search teams to establish adoptions for Polish children. DP camp officials used that process to repatriate other children, including those of us from the Baltics.

To set the process in motion, the UNRRA instructed Dr. Bergfelde to split us according to nationality, have her staff photograph us, and attach short biographies to each picture.[11]

The first efforts at returning some children to Latvia went well. Orphanage officials handed over four children after Latvian parents presented documents proving they were the natural parents. Soviet repatriation generals received those children. Polish officials accepted eleven children for Polish repatriation a year later.

But then a disturbing practice began to take place—adoption. It would ultimately backfire. One of the caretakers at the Latvian DP camp, A. Zvēriņš, described how it happened:[12]

> In the beginning Latvian Red Cross had some power, and it began adoption of children into Latvian families. Some people from UNRRA got really angry about it and demanded those children to be returned to the orphanage. Foster parents who had already fallen in love with the children, had to return them. After some time IRO began adoption for Latvian families again, but the procedure was very complicated, and only about 10 children got adopted in Latvian families.

These actions were, in the words of Marvin Klemmé,[13]

> a disgrace to both organization and to humanity . . .
> As long as they were helping to reunite families it was

all right, but in the end many of them spent more time breaking up families.

This action outraged many groups who had wanted to send us back to our homeland, regardless of its politics. Sereny went on to explain her concern:

> How could anyone think of ordering that children who had twice suffered the trauma of losing parents, home, and language, should, like so many packages, be transported overseas and dropped into yet other new and entirely strange environments?

Critics of adoption argued that children were now traumatized twice, first by being separated from their birth parents and then again from their foster parents. Any kind of repatriation—whether it involved biological or adoptive parents—was out of the question. One caregiver, E. Plūme, wrote with a tone of resignation, "Despite the efforts of one Latvian organization to return Latvian children to their parents, the military council didn't find it necessary to return them to their families."[14]

Although Communist officials were outraged by British schemes to resettle displaced East European youth in the United States, Canada, or Australia, they knew they were in no position to help Latvian parents or relatives reclaim their children. Soviets had already listed our names in its newspaper, *Aicinajums Cīņa*, in the hopes that some parents who recognized the names of their children would come forward to claim them.

I wondered about that *Cīņa* list. There were questions for which I would never find the answer. How many parents were reunited with their children as a result of seeing their child's name on it? Most important of all, why did my family never see it?

Transatlantic adoptions came to the fore. Not only did advocates for it argue that adoptions would keep children out from under the influence of Communism, they also felt that as children, we were "more assimilable" than adults. In the end, the IRO reported that of the nearly seventeen thousand registered unaccompanied children in the British and American Zones, only a thousand were reunited with relatives. Most other were repatriated or resettled abroad.[15]

This seesaw battle over repatriation and adoption was only one of two moving parts in this refugee crisis. The country to which most refugees wished to go—the United States—had its own set of unresolved conflicts. It had restrictive immigration policies. Both the government and citizens were opposed to accepting immigrants, adults or children.

US Immigration Policy

British and American charitable organizations knew how strong US public sentiment was against taking in refugees, adults as well as children. Not only would it take years to resolve the issue of repatriation, but it would take years to change the attitudes of the American public on immigration.

Unwillingness to accept Eastern European refugees was rooted decades earlier in the "popular disillusionment with conflict-ridden Europe in the aftermath of the First World War."[16] The US Congress introduced quota systems then, which allowed only a limited number of immigrants from Southern and Eastern Europe. The harshest measure was directed against the Asians. None could apply.

The US Congress struggled over its immigration policy for three years. Harry N. Rosenfield, acting chairman of the displaced persons commission, said, "We don't want any security risks—anyone who is a Commie or a Nazi—coming into the United States under the DP program." There was also a strong anti-Jewish sentiment.[17]

It would take several events to turn around public sentiment, as well as the attitudes of US congressmen. One activist group that took on that mission was the Citizens Committee for Displaced Persons, headed by Earl Harrison. President Truman asked him to assess the status of displaced persons in Germany, especially Jews.

After touring the camps, he issued the Harrison Report, demanding significant improvements in camp conditions. He called for immediate help for Jews to leave Germany and Austria and to immigrate to

MARIJA PLATACE FUTCHS FINE

the United States and British-held Palestine. Most importantly, he influenced Representative William G. Stratton of Illinois to introduce the first DP bill in April 1947.

The desire to keep out war criminals—whether Nazi or Communist—proved unsuccessful. Boļeslavs Maikovskis and Konrāds Kalējs, both of whom were possibly behind the path of persecution of my family and that of thousands of others, slipped into the United States under the guise of being refugees.

They were among the eighty percent who were Christian. The smaller number—one in five—were Jewish. The Citizens Committee recognized that in order for America to admit one hundred thousand Jews, it was necessary to allow four times that number of DPs into the country. This inevitably meant allowing in some Nazi collaborators, but the Committee believed that it was a risk they had to take.

Visits to DP camps by some prominent congressmen helped shape public opinion. But it was the films and radio programs that addressed the topic that undoubtedly made the greatest impact on how Americans learned about events in Europe. People learned about the Communist coup in Czechoslovakia, the Berlin Airlift, and the Marshall Plan. 1948 was called "the year Hollywood brought the Cold War to Main Street America."

In the same year, after a bitter fight in Congress, the United States finally passed the Displaced Persons Act and promised, starting in October of that year, to take ten thousand refugees a month from Europe. The wave of immigrants began in 1949, when forty thousand DPs reached the United States. Eventually, the United States accepted more than four hundred thousand refugees from the European camps.

The British military council gave the director of the Latvian DP camp, Tērmanis, the orders that Lutheran children would go to the USA, and Catholics to Canada. This was—as I reviewed the records— an interesting development. It is but one of those examples of how the unpredictable hand of fate enters our lives.

Even though I was christened a Roman Catholic, that did not show up on my orphanage record. Since I was christened a Lutheran two years after I arrived in Hahnenklee, I have that unnamed Lutheran pastor to thank for my going to America.

Caretakers prepared us for the flight we would take out of Hamburg. That included one final act for my friends, the Leviņš twins. E. Plüme, a caretaker in the Kinder Haus, wrote about them in the article "For the Sake of Truth" in *Latvija Amerikā*:[18]

> So Andris and Mirdza, accompanied by their caretaker,
> a few days before flying to the USA, went to the nearby
> town of Goslar to say goodbye to their parents' graves.

The Lutherans

The Lutheran World Federation was one of the charitable organizations that set the stage for sending war refugees into America. Lutherans felt a commitment to its members, realizing one in three Latvian displaced refugees in Europe was Lutheran.[19]

The Lutheran church started to find homes and employment for one hundred eighty-five thousand Baltic Lutherans. The National Lutheran Council (NLC) and the Lutheran World Federation worked in tandem to allow Lutherans in the United States to adopt Lutheran war orphans or sponsor Lutheran families.

Persuading Lutheran families to accept Latvian émigrés required a media outreach campaign. The NLC sent Pastor Ross Hidy of Richmond, California, to Germany to film a Latvian family in Valka-Lager DP Camp in Nuremburg. That provided key film footage for the 1949 film *Answer for Anne*, aimed at encouraging Lutheran congregations to sponsor Latvian refugees. The film showed a young American student, Anne, posing the question to townspeople about their receptiveness to accepting immigrants.

Ross Hidy continued his involvement by making the adoption arrangements for all Lutheran orphans, mostly to Lutheran ministers' families in the United States. While he was in Germany, he chose the two children he and his wife, Evelyn, would adopt, fraternal twins

Andris and Mirdza. They chose American names Drew and Marilyn, which were close approximations of their Latvian names.

Seventy of us arrived on a Transocean flight on March 15, 1949, from Hamburg via Iceland through the auspices of the Quaker American Friends Service Committee, which operated on a nonsectarian basis.[20]

After the twenty-three staff members of the Hahnenklee orphanage left for new homes in America, Canada, and Australia, they wrote reports of their views about the evacuation of their former charges, the orphans. The attitude of one expressed wistfulness and a sense of resignation about it:[21]

> Even though it's sad, we must accept that these children are lost to Latvians. The only comfort is to know that they are saved from Communist slavery and will have good upbringing, parents' love and will grow up to be free citizens of the USA. After the long and torturous journey they came to the British zone and were administered by UNRRA.

In the end, families in the United States, Israel, and Canada adopted four thousand of us, including most who had lived at Golf Hotel/Kinder Haus. When the Displaced Persons Act finally expired in 1952, a total of 381,000 people entered the United States under its provisions. The United States took forty percent of the total number of all refugees.[22]

The Carl Futchs Family, Jersey City, New Jersey
Photos from Futchs family album

With Aunts Ave and Jo
and adoptive mother
Selma, 1949

In the front yard of the
Carl Futchs home, April 1949

List of Children in Rīga Newspaper *Cīņa*[1]

(*Fight*, November 30, 1947)

Bērnu vecākus vai personas, kas zinātu par bērnu vecākiem, lūdz pieteikties personīgi vai rakstiski LPSR Ministru Padomes repatriācijas nodaļā Brīvības bulvārī 10 vai «Cīņas» redakcijā Blaumaņa ielā 38/40 10. istabā pie techniskajām sekretārēm.

(Translation: The children's parents or persons who know about the children's parents, please apply in person or in writing to the Council of Ministers of the Latvia Chapter of Freedom Repatriation Boulevard 10 battles or Blaumana Street 38/40 10. Room for technical staff of secretaries.)

(The highlighted names are the fraternal twins Andris and Mirdza, no. 31 and no. 32, and myself no. 70 on the list.)

1. Adijans Anna, 8 g. v., aizvesta no Baldones bērnu nama;
2. Andrejevs, 3,5 g. v., aizvests no Kapseļu ielas bērnu nama;
3. Asars-Asaris Jānis, 8 g. v., aizvests no Kapseļu ielas bērnu nama;
4. Balodis Jānis, 3,5 g. v., aizvests no Kapseļu ielas bērnu nama;
5. Bergmans Jānis, 5 g. v., aizvests no Kapseļu ielas bērnu nama;
6. Birznieks-Feldmanis Pēteris, 4 g. v., aizvests no Kapseļu ielas bērnu nama;
7. Blūmītis Valdis, 4 g. v.;
8. Bogdanova Valda, 4,5 g. v., aizvesta no Kapseļu ielas bērnu nama;
9. Brūvers Jānis, 4,5 g. v., aizvests no Kapseļu ielas bērnu nama;
10. Blaževics Heinrichs, 3 g. v., aizvests no Kapseļu ielas bērnu nama;
11. Bumbiers Eduards, 6,5 g. v., aizvests no Kapseļu ielas bērnu nama;
12. Burovs Sergejs, 3,5 g. v., aizvests no Kapseļu ielas bērnu nama;
13. Cīrulis Dzidra Malvīne, 4,5 g. v., aizvesta no Kapseļu ielas bērnu nama;
14. Dainis Kārlis, 4,5 g. v., aizvests no Kapseļu ielas bērnu nama;
15. Dreijers Valija, 5 g. v., aizvesta no Kapseļu ielas bērnu nama;

[1]   Website: http://rīgacv.lv, posted 2010.

16. Dreijers Vilis, 6,5 g. v., aizvests no Kapseļu ielas bērnu nama (brālis un māsa);
17. Ēķis Harijs, 5 g. v.;
18. Freimanis Jēkabs, 6 g. v., aizvests no Kapseļu ielas bērnu nama;
19. Jegilovičs, 5 g. v., aizvests no Kapseļu ielas bērnu nama;
20. Jumis Liliana, 4. g. v., aizvesta no Kapseļu ielas bērnu nama;
21. Kalniņš Ivars, 5 g. v., mātesbrālis un māsa — ģimnāziste no Rīgas bieži apmeklēja bērnu un gribēja viņu aizvest sev līdzi;
22. Kazimirenko Elza, 4,5 g. v., aizvesta no Kapseļu ielas bērnu nama;
23. Kercis Imants, 7 g. v., aizvests no Kapseļu ielas bērnu nama;
24. Kubeckis Pāvels, 5 g. v., aizvests no Kapseļu ielas bērnu nama;
25. Kuprišova Valija, 3,5 g. v., aizvesta no Kapseļu ielas bērnu nama;
26. Kurša Austra, 6 g. v., aizvesta no Kapseļu ielas bērnu nama;
27. Laizāns Grigorijs, 3,5 g. v., aizvests no Kapseļu ielas bērnu nama;
28. Lakotkins Eduards, 4 g. v.;
29. Kreišmanis Erna, 4 g. v., aizvesta no Kapseļu ielas bērnu nama;
30. Ļebedevs Nikolajs, 4,5 g. v., aizvests no Kapseļu ielas bērnu nama;
31. **Leviņš Andris, 6 g. v.,**
32. **Leviņš Mirdza, 6 g. v., — dvīņi, aizvesti no Kapseļu ielas bērnu nama;**
33. Ludvigs Bruno, 4,5 g. v.;
34. Lunaitis Alfrēds, 5 g. v.; aizvests no Kapseļu ielas bērnu nama;
35. Maculcviča Viktorija, 3,5 g. v., aizvesta no Kapseļu ielas bērnu nama;
36. Mikulane Lidija, 4 g. v.;
37. Muižnieks Ādolfs, 3,5 g. v., aizvests no Kapseļu ielas bērnu nama;
38. Namatēvs Jānis, 5,5 g. v., aizvests no Kapseļu ielas bērnu nama;
39. Nikolajevs Juris, 5,5 g. v., aizvests no Kapseļu ielas bērnu nama;
40. Netie Imants, 5,5 g. v., aizvests no Valmieras;
41. Ozoliņa Astride, 4,5 g. v., aizvesta no Valmieras bērnu nama;
42. Ozoliņš Juris,4,5 g. v., aizvests no Valmieras bērnu nama;
43. Paeglīte Vizbulīte, 4,5 g. v., aizvesta no Valmieras bērnu nama;
44. Piskunovs Nikolajs, 5 g. v., aizvests no Valmieras bērnu nama;

MARIJA PLATACE FUTCHS FINE

45. Pūce Ilmārs, 5,5 g. v., aizvests no Valmieras bērnu nama;
46. Puskundziņš Jāzeps, 4,5 g. v., aizvests no Valmieras bērnu nama;
47. Rebane Gunārs, 5 g. v., aizvests no Valmieras bērnu nama;
48. Resnacis Vilnis, 5,5 g. v., aizvests no Valmieras bērnu nama;
49. Skalders Jānis, 4,5 g. v., aizvests no Valmieras bērnu nama;
50. Skripka Māra-Zinaida, 3,5 g. v., aizvesta no Valmieras bērnu nama;
51. Ščepulenoks Jānis, 7,5 g. v., aizvests no Valmieras bērnu nama:
52. Subotjalo Pēteris, 5 g. v., aizvests no Valmieras bērnu nama;
53. Švarcbachs Rūdolfs, 3,5 g. v., aizvests no Valmieras bērnu nama;
54. Sakals Alfrēds, 6,5 g. v., aizvests no Baldones bērnu nama;
55. Tichomirova Anita, 5 g. v., aizvesta no Kapseļu ielas bērnu nama;
56. Valenieks Gunārs, 3 g. v., aizvests no Kapseļu ielas bērnu nama;
57. Zacenskis Jānis, 6 g. v., aizvests no Kapseļu ielas bērnu nama;
58. Zaļums Alfrēds, 5,5 g. v. aizvests no Kapseļu ielas bērnu nama;
59. Zamcičs Anita, 4 g. v., aizvesta no Kapseļu ielas bērnu nama;
60. Zasnis Valda, 3,5 g. v., aizvesta no Kapseļu ielas bērnu nama;
61. Zīmulis Guntis, 5 g. v., aizvests no Kapseļu ielas bērnu nama;
62. Zēbergs Jāņis, 5 g. v., aizvests no Kapseļu ielas bērnu nama;
63. Amantovs Daumanis, 6 g. v., aizvests no Kapseļu ielas bērnu nama;
64. Andrejeva Aleksandra, 4 g. v., aizvesta no Salaspils koncentrācijas nometnes;
65. Draugaveika Jekaterina, 4 g. v., aizvesta no Salaspils koncentrācijas nometnes;
66. Igorčenko Nikolajs, 3,5 g. v., no Salaspils koncentrācijas nometnes;
67. Korsaks Voldemārs, 3,5 g. v., no Salaspils koncentrācijas nometnes;
68. Kupčiks Anatolijs, 3 g. v., no Salaspils koncentrācijas nometnes;
69. Naporova Tatjana, 3,5 g. v., no Salaspils koncentrācijas nometnes;
70. **Platačs Marija, 4 g. v., no Salaspils koncentrācijas nometnes;**
71. Tirāns Natalija, 3,5 g. v., no Salaspils koncentrācijas nometnes;

CHAPTER 13

Marija Platača's Life

They Are Forming Kolkhozes Everywhere

A S THE TRANSOCEAN flight swept me up into the air on March 15, 1949, Marija Platača disappeared into the clouds. Five months later, I became Mariya Futchs.

But what if someone in my family had seen the article in *Cīņa*, the newspaper that listed my name as one of the missing Latvian children the Soviets wanted to bring back to Latvia? What if I had been reunited with my parents? The story might have turned out something like the following:

As my father's brother Vitālijs read the November 1947 issue of Aicinajums Cīņa, *he saw an article that electrified him. It listed the names of missing children for family to claim at the Council of Ministers in Rīga. He recognized my name and went posthaste to his brother in Dobele.*

Broņislavs agreed that all the identifiers—name, Salaspils, age— matched what he knew about me. Within weeks, the British military, Red Cross, and DP camp officials sent me into my father's welcoming arms.

Although this happened eleven months after my parents divorced, neither one had remarried. Would my father try again to win back Solomeja? Yes. Being a confident man who still loved her, he telephoned with the good news. Both he and I would meet her in Virauda, where she was living with her infant child.

That gave my mother time to take it all in. She was conflicted. While she was excited at the thought of seeing me, she still blamed my father for the time she spent in concentration camps. In the end, she decided to reunite with him. She realized that the man she blamed for losing me was the man who was now returning me to her.

Our first meeting was joyous and tense at the same time. My mother was stunned to see I was now a child of four years and six months, walking and speaking Latvian. Although I was dazed by it all, I welcomed it. I knew how to adapt, having moved so often and having to adjust to so many different places.

Days before our family reunion, my father and I bonded with our love of music. I learned many songs in the orphanage, which I loved singing for him and with him. His eyes lit up when I sang the traditional Latvian folksong "Rīga dimd." I had by then developed very strong vocal chords and a penchant for showing off. So I didn't need much encouragement to sing it for my parents:[1]

> Rīga resounds, Rīga resounds
> Who made Rīga so resound?
> Aijaijā Tralalā
> Who made Rīga so resound?

The sound of Aijaijā Tralalā was always so thrilling to me that I just kept repeating it, getting louder each time I sang it. My father broke in to say, "Wonderful! Now, can you sing us another song? Maybe a slower one?" He was sorry he didn't bring his accordion. But we would change all that when we three returned to Dobele. We would have song sessions like the ones my father enjoyed while he was growing up.

After we returned to Dobele, my mother joined a nearby kolkhoz. Unlike other family members who took up new occupations after the war, she stayed with farming. It was all she knew. However, she was unhappy that she was no longer working alongside family members, but instead with strangers in a communal system.

In1946 Soviets started collectivizing the privately owned farms that people such as the Platacis family had known for three generations.[2] Many farmers migrated from the countryside to the towns and cities to pursue other kinds of livelihood. Both my father and Vitālijs became policemen.

Since my father had only a fifth-grade education, he left Rīga after six months and took on work as a carpenter and beekeeper. He was a self-taught man. He learned how to be a beekeeper by reading a fix-it-yourself guide.

Vitālijs, the most educated member of the family, enrolled in law enforcement courses to move up through the ranks as a police officer. I had a girlhood crush on him. He looked so strong and handsome, especially when he wore his policeman's uniform.

Other family members changed their roles even before the war ended. Younger members such as Leonora and her siblings assumed adult responsibility by taking over the family farm in the absence her parents. Tante Leonora continued her studies to become a nurse in Rīga, where Malvīna worked in a factory. Even Grandmother Helēna managed the farm for a while until she was forced to give it up.

When my father saw that I did well with reading and writing, he wanted me to continue my studies, all the way to a university in Rīga, if that's what I wanted to do. Until that time, I remained in Dobele with my parents and my infant brother, Andris. We lived in the home my father had just built, very much like the one he built for us in Rusiški four years earlier. He built a barn where he did his woodwork and separate living quarters, which had one floor and an attic.

My father took me under his wing, showing me—just as his father did—how he worked at his trade. He took me to the one place he loved, the forest. He taught me that Latvia's green gold was its timber, whose varieties ranged from oak, pine, black and common alder, larch, spruce, aspen, to birch.[3]

When I went into the forest with him and Vitālijs, I watched them cut down trees. We went on a tractor that Broņislavs drove. We were equipped with our ax, handsaws, and a giant rope that would brace the men up against a tree as they drove wedges into its massive trunk. They figured out from what angle to cut the tree. My father was so full of confidence that he picked one of the more challenging trees, the birch.[4]

They used a rope pulley system. Vitālijs made the first 45 degree wedges into the tree with a hammer, then used an ax to begin chopping into the wood. All the while we shielded our eyes as the chunks and splinters of wood scattered in all directions.

MARIJA PLATACE FUTCHS FINE

My dad and Vitālijs took out the handsaw and took turns cutting back and forth with handsaws. Even though Vitālijs was as tall as my father was short, they worked out the right kind of balance between them.

It was as exciting as it was scary to hear the cracking sound as the tree split from its trunk. Sometimes a birch tree was curled or had big branches on one side, making its fall less predictable. It was always a guessing game: How would it fall? Would it roll back and forth, or rotate as it crashed down? Would it bounce away, even slam sideways? Or would its thorny braces get hung up in neighboring trees?

Once the tree was on the ground, the brothers cut it into logs and lifted them onto the tractor with huge tongs. After we arrived home, I'd watch how they cut the logs into boards.

As I watched my father use his hands to craft a sled or a crib, I admired the compact, precise movements he used. Those were the times he taught me even more songs, especially ones that celebrated nature. He asked me to practice playing a variety of musical instruments as he created so many wonderful pieces of furniture and other items they would sell at the market.

At every opportunity, I drew as many people around me to sing as I played the mandolin or balalaika. In no time, I became the song leader for my group, which competed in the grand song competitions in Rīga when thousands from around the country performed dainas and other well-known songs.

Just as I formed a special kinship with my father, I also formed a special one with my mother. It was a bittersweet connection that our prison and camp experience gave us. But anytime I asked her about the prison and camps, she would have that faraway look and would change the subject.

I grieved with her when little brother Andris died; he was only eighteen months old. He never knew a healthy day in his short life. It was just the three of us for a time. But over the years, my mother and father grew apart.

Her imprisonment had dealt so grievous an assault to her psyche that she could not overcome it. Something shattered inside my mother that could never be made whole again. They remained married in name only. Solomeja stayed with a Danovksa cousin in a separate house that was close to her kolkhoz.

I entered the Jāzeps Vītols Latvian Conservatory[5] in 1961 to pursue music studies, with the thought of becoming a concert soloist. While pursuing my university education, I stayed with Uncle Vitālijs and his wife and daughter in their Rīga flat since Leonora's flat was filled. The seven of them were squeezed in together: husband Gūnars and their firstborn, Helēna and sister Malvīna, whose family, husband, and newborn lived in the kitchen.

Leonora told me about the class assignment that ended her dream of becoming a nurse. She and other students had to study the cut-open stomach of a corpse on the table in a morgue, far too gruesome for her. She took up tailoring, which prompted me to ask her to sew dresses for me, just as she knitted my stockings when I was a baby. I wore her dresses for the recitals I performed in.

I met my husband at the university, whom everyone regarded as a rising star in the world of music. And indeed, he went on to become a noted composer in the '70s. He was someone who was like my father: handsome, musically gifted, confident, blessed with a wonderful sense of humor, and a very loving individual.

Whenever I returned from Rīga to Dobele during class breaks, I went to the kolkhoz to meet my mother just before her workday ended. We went back to her home where I would experience the kind of individual she was through her farming.

She told me everything about how to milk a cow.[6] "I start by cleaning the bucket, and everything else that comes into contact with the milk," she said. "I feed her, clean the manger, and give her silage and water." She stressed the importance of having a gentle but firm grip when pumping the milk out of the teats. She also explained how, when she first started to hand-milk as a young girl, it was such hard work that her arms began to burn.

So I asked her, "Couldn't you do anything about that?"

She answered, "I did it often enough that I developed muscles in my hands and forearms. That made it easier to hand-milk. Sometimes—back in Andrupene—I placed my hands against the cold stone wall to cool down the burn I felt in my hands."

My mother loved cows so much that she had names for each one she milked. She had a story for just about every cow as well. She had to tie back

Zanda's hind legs because she was so anxious; that was the only way to keep her calm when she milked her. Her favorite, though, was Grieta. As my mother caressed her neck, Grieta would lick her hand in grateful response.

Her favorite cow story was about Venta,[7] who actually belonged to her uncle Kazimirs, my great-uncle. She liked telling the story because she found one more reason to appreciate the fact that she and my father had chosen one of his two daughters, Monika, to be my godmother at my christening ceremony. She showed herself to be clever, strong, and caring.

When Germans raided her uncle's farm during their occupation, they took everything but two sheep and Venta. When the Russians came back, the collectivized farm system swallowed up the Platacis farms, including the one Kazimirs owned. When it came time for the family to leave Andrupene for their new life in Veselava, daughters Monika and Janīna didn't want to leave Venta behind.

I asked my mother, "Where is Veselava?"

She said, "It's in Vidzeme, northern Latvia, one hundred twenty-four miles from Andrupene."

It amazed me that two young girls would take Venta on so long a journey by themselves. Monika was sixteen; her younger sister, twelve. My mother agreed that it would take days, since they would be on foot the entire time.

Moreover, she said the world was not a safe place after the war. Partisans were still hiding in the woods.

"Partisans? You mean like father?"[8] I asked my mother.

"Not exactly. There are different kinds of partisans. Your father was a Soviet partisan. These are nationalists. They want a free Latvia."

"Isn't that a good thing? You and father say you want a free Latvia, don't you?" I asked.

"Yes, of course, but not everyone supports the partisans. Many don't want to give them food to survive, which the partisans need since they hide out in forests, where they have nothing to eat. Some of them go into farms and steal animals or food. Some of them even kill people in the farms."

Mother said cows weren't safe either on the kind of journey my aunts were taking. People would steal them, or they could fall ill on the trip. You couldn't call people on a phone for help. A phone was a rare thing to find in the country in the first place, and even if you made a call, there probably was no one on the other end to receive the call.

But Kazimirs and Jadviga trusted their daughters, who were very responsible. They knew Venta would provide both a source of food for them and money for their lodging on the five-day journey. They gave them bread for additional sustenance.

Monika and Janīna traveled on a gravel road, which was hard on their feet since they were walking in rubber shoes. After about twenty miles, they saw travelers sitting in a cart with a cow tied to it. The cow was sleeping in the middle of the road. Monika asked, "What happened to your cow? Is it sick?"

The man answered, "You could say that. But after fifteen miles, the cow is done. The truth is, its legs are damaged from the road, and it just refused to walk on."

Monika asked, "What do you plan to do now that your cow can't walk?'"

"We'll let her rest until the morning," the man answered, "and then we'll see. If she can't walk then, we'll have to sell her. Such a shame. Although small, she was a good cow. Yours, however, is big and fat, a proper milk cow!"

"Yes," replied Monika, "That is why we're taking her to Veselava." As she said this, she secretly thought, Let's get moving. They are jealous of our cow.

After that conversation, they had Venta walk on the grassy side of the road. They covered eighteen miles the first day.

They came to a house where the lady allowed them to sleep in her barn without paying. Even though they didn't have to give her anything, the sisters wanted to do something for her. They offered to cut the grass in her field with a scythe that she provided for them. The woman was stunned that the two girls' parents allowed them to take the cow on their own for so many miles. She warned them, "You can't trust anyone after the war."

The girls hit their stride on the second day, covering thirty-one miles. Despite the hardship Venta endured, she delivered milk on a frequent basis. They were able to get milk out of her even after eight hours.

At the end of the second day, they met Olga and her husband, Roberts, who welcomed the girls to stay in their home. But something was not right about this couple. While Olga was friendly, they couldn't say the same about her husband. Both kept saying they wanted to buy Venta several times, but each time, Monika and Jānina said they would not sell her. They would only give them milk to pay for their overnight stay.

While they were in their room, the girls overheard Olga warning her husband that the girls wouldn't give up Venta. He responded, "Stop worrying about the cow. It'll be yours in the morning."

Olga asked, "How do you intend to do that?"

Robert answered in his gruff manner, "That ain't your business or a matter for your soft heart." Robert was up to something, and the girls didn't like it.

Monika and Jānina had breakfast with the couple, enjoying the bread, pickles, and onion. After the meal, they noticed Roberts went out to the barn and started pulling at the rope around Venta's neck, which, Monika could see, frightened Venta.

Monika rushed out to the barn and started to seize the rope from Roberts, refusing to let go. They were now in a tugging match with the rope between them. Jānina started crying as she saw her sister struggle with Roberts. Hard as it was for Monika, she was glad she had performed so many strenuous farm duties, which made her quite strong for a girl. Even so, the tug-of-war hurt her hands, but she would fight to keep Roberts from taking Venta away.

Suddenly the family froze. An old dog ran into the yard, and Robert fled into the house. "Old Antons is coming so early," Olga said to the girls. "Go, get out of here!"

Monika and Jānina didn't need any encouragement. They ran away as fast as they could, pulling Venta along with them. It was not just to save Venta but also to avoid the dog, which they thought might start chasing after them.

As the girls moved along the road, Venta mooed at other cows in the field.

A gypsy family approached them. There was someone in the group who didn't look like she belonged with them, a blond girl. She came up to them, declaring, "We want milk!" Almost in the same breath, she asked, "Are you interested in selling the cow? We can give dresses and nice jewelry in exchange for her."

Both Monika and Janīna answered unison, "No!"

The gypsies brought out a clean bucket, and Venta produced milk for them. Monika was surprised at how clean the bucket was, because gypsies had a reputation for being unclean. As Monika milked Venta, she saw children tugging at their mother's dress. One jumped around her, almost climbing on top of her.

The sisters asked the blond girl what she was doing with these gypsies. She explained that after her father was killed in the war, the gypsy family came upon her and her mother and began to take care of them. She then warned them about sleeping outdoors. "It's dangerous, with the partisans and robbers. They kill livestock. They could kill you too."

Hours later, a man they passed alongside the road saw Monika reading a book and asked if she was going to Rīga for more studies. As my mother mentioned this, she stopped, looked at me, and said, "I want you to be like Monika and Leonora. Go on with your studies. I finished only three grades, so I'm stuck with farmwork. You don't have to be like me."

That night, the sisters had to sleep on the side of the road, hoping they wouldn't run into bandits. As they awakened, a man showed up on a large horse. In a commanding voice, he said, "Fill in a protocol. I am going to confiscate your cow! You are on my land."

But just as quickly, he laughed and said, "Just joking. It won't be my land for much longer. It will be a kolkhoz. I have one life to live, and they expect me to spend it on a kolkhoz? They are forming kolkhozes everywhere."

I asked my mother, "What's a protocol?"

She explained, "A protocol is a written agreement, an official paper."

Monika told the man she understood how he felt. "We're going to join our father because our land was taken away and given to the state."

On the fourth day, Monika and Janīna met Leva, a widow who said they could stay the night in her home. She was alone, as she lost both her husband and her son in the war. Even though she had a cow, she accepted Venta's milk as payment for their stay. They had fresh potato and herring for supper, which was, again, a welcome change from the dull ration of bread.

In the middle of the night, the sisters heard shots ring out. Within moments, Leva entered their room and said, "It must be partisans robbing farmers of their cattle. They need to eat meat, which they cannot get in the forest." She told them to pick up their belongings and go with her and the two cows behind the granary. She cautioned them to do their best to keep the cows quiet.

Though they were well hidden, Monika and Jānina could overhear the two men. The one said to the other, "I think this a widow whose son never came back from the war. She has a cow. I've seen it."

The other one answered, "That's a hassle. Let's see if she has some chickens in the barn. Catching them is gonna make a lot of noise, though."

Moments later, they heard one say, "Damn, this pig is heavy. You, Zigis, take something. Go and see the chickens!"

When Zigis got to the barn, he said, "I won't go there in the dark, might step into some shit!"

Everyone remained silent until the men disappeared with Ieva's pig. When the coast was clear, everyone joined in a chorus of "Thank God."

Leva's neighbor wasn't so lucky. A friend of the neighbor came over to tell Leva and the Platacis sisters the men punched the neighbor in the stomach, which sent him to the hospital. They reported it to the militia, who chased after them in the Madona forest and captured them.

I think my mother liked this story because she appreciated how important Venta was to her nieces. They were willing to take her on the long and dangerous journey because they valued her more than any price anyone could offer them for her.

While my imagined life is interesting to contemplate, it means more just knowing the one true thing about my parents. My mother and father loved me. Solomeja fought against guards to hold on to me, and Broņislavs spent years searching for me. Realizing their love is a feeling I will carry for the rest of my life.

My Arrival in the USA, March 1949
Photos courtesy of Pathé

John and Selma Futchs, 1945 Wedding
Futchs Family Album

The birth certificate prepared weeks
after my arrival, April 1949

Birth certificate issued by the Embassy of
the Republic of Latvia, May 2014
Photos by Marija Platace Futchs Fine

CHAPTER 14

Adoption

Tired, Wan, Broken Little
Old Men and Women

War Waifs

H ISTORIAN TARA ZAHRA observed that the entry of war orphans in the United States in 1949 "profoundly shaped the practice of international adoption in the decades that followed. International adoption was itself a major legacy of World War II."[1] Americans had never before seen such a massive influx of foreign child refugees as it experienced in that year.

We brought a host of new issues for our adoptive parents, many of whom wondered how international institutional care would affect our cultural adaptation, linguistic development, and behavior. Many assumed the worst.

UNRRA welfare worker Eileen Davidson, viewed those of us "who had been removed from German institutions . . . bore the telltale signs of authoritarian Nazi behavior." She went on to say,[2]

> These children are apparently subjected to rigid routines and discipline and ordinarily they are shy, extremely fearful, and do not know how to play, even amongst themselves. Their behavior is that of very repressed children, and it is in marked contrast to the behavior of children in this group who have been with us any length

of time who ordinarily are extremely friendly to adults, very active and free in their play and activities.

Perhaps the most poignant description of us came from an aid worker who said we were "tired, wan, broken little old men and women," who had "forgotten—or never knew—how to play."[3]

Even one of our Latvian caretakers who flew over as a refugee to the United States described some of the orphans as *defective*, a lingering term associated with eugenics. He wrote,[4]

> Children taken to the USA first ended in an orphanage in New York, where some caretakers were also Latvians. Parents wishing to adopt children were scrupulously checked for material status, moral character, etc. Almost all children have been adopted, except for some defective children who are taken to special care and education institutions.

But words such as *tired*, *wan*, and *broken* didn't apply to many orphans, certainly not to me. When I arrived at Jersey City, New Jersey, I joined other unaccompanied children and refugee families at a settlement run by Pastor Carl Futchs, the social secretary of the New Jersey Lutheran Social Services. His home was on the campus that had dormitories where all of us stayed before going to our new homes.

Carl Futchs had agreed to find a child for his brother John and his wife, Selma. The amount of time and the paperwork involved in my adoption was comparatively simple compared to what it is nowadays. My future aunt and uncle would choose either a boy or a girl for my father from the group of orphans who flew into New York that day in March 1949.

Aunt Ave

My American aunt, Ave Futchs, described us in the first session she and her husband Carl had with three of us, two girls and a boy. From the sound of her letter, we seemed to be reasonably well adjusted. Aunt Ave wrote the following account on March 27, 1949. [It appears verbatim, retaining the spelling, capitalization, and internal punctuation of the original letter.] [5]

Dear John and Selma:

Yesterday morning Carl and I had an experience we wish you might have had, rather than our having it for you. Mary Winston[6] had made an appointment for us to see three children with the idea of choosing the one we thot [*sp*] would best fit your need and love. The boy was fine, and will have fine possibilities I'm sure, but is very independent and you'd miss the dependence and cuddlesomness. Between the two little girls we could hardly choose at first, as both were alert and friendly and attractive. Neither is a beauty, but both have pleasing features and with the proper clothes and haircuts will be very attractive. Both had outsize clothing on. We were with them in the interview room over an hour and watched them play, both with the others and on our laps. At first Carl leaned to the one he had on his lap much of the time, and she is loveable, but the one I had suited me so much. She was affectionate and quick, but not slobbery about her affection. For short periods she would go off on concerns of her own to play absorbedly with my scarf in a truck, for instance. But she came back oftener and oftener to be held on my lap to play. However, when we left she accepted it well. These poor youngsters aren't used to good things lasting too long, I guess, including visitors. Both girls speak only Latvi/ean but it was surprising how quickly we established communications. At one time Carl noticed that Mariya (the one we took to most) had her shoestrings open. She immediately bent down and did a workmanlike job to

MARIJA PLATACE FUTCHS FINE

tying them. I think both girls are around 4 1/2 to 6—I would think Mariya to be about 5 or under. You may have the full data on her by the time you get this letter, but since it was to be sent to the agency there, perhaps this will reach you first, and besides, I am sure you want as many details to round out the picture as we can give. Mariya's name is said by her and her playmates very much like we say Maria with more of an accent on the first syllable. Mar'-ee-ya. One can't find out too much in so short a time, but we surely watched the children like hawks to see how they would take sharing toys and interference with play, etc. We think you could be very, very happy with either little girl, and especially with Mariya, and feel she would surely be happy with you. We surely hope that this is your little daughter. We could surely love her, I'm sure."

Days after Ave wrote this letter, my adoptive mother arrived by train from Boulder, Colorado, to the Futchs family home in New Jersey. It was love at first sight for mother and daughter. We took to each other instantly.

We traveled by train to Colorado, where my father stood by at the station with a cameramen from the local paper who take a picture of the new family. My motion sickness throughout the train journey ruined my Kodak moment. As my parents beamed at me, I could only manage a sour expression. John and Selma Futchs officially adopted me on August 2, 1950.

Though everyone received me warmly in New Jersey and Colorado, Americans reacted to unaccompanied minors with mixed emotions. Those reactions reflected the political and social realities of the day. Historian Tara Zahra said our presence had "a special grip on the postwar imagination," embodying, as we did, "Europeans' most ambitious hopes and their deepest fears about the future in 1945."[7]

Some Americans felt we reflected the quintessential wartime tragedy and legacy of the Second World War, the "familial separation," a phenomenon that psychologists saw as a form of psychic trauma. The very concept of trauma had changed over the years. Zahra outlined the evolution of the term *trauma*:[8]

> The concept of trauma had first been defined as a neurological condition in Great Britain in the 1860s and 1870s, when it was used to describe the disturbing symptoms afflicting early railroad travelers, including headaches, vertigo, sleep disorders, ill temper, paralysis, and impotence. From its origins, trauma was thus associated with displacement. Initially considered a result of injuries to the nervous system, in the 1880s continental psychiatrists, such as Jean-Martin Martin Charcot in France and Hermann Oppenheim in Germany, developed a view of trauma as a psychological or emotional condition akin to hysteria or neurosis.

From the 1940s up through the 1990s, researchers and social policy makers studied the developmental impact of institutionalization of orphans. They focused on whether poor developmental beginnings affected children growing up in orphanages in Iran, Lebanon, Greece, Romania, Russia, Canada, and the United States.[9]

The earliest studies began in the war years, the 1940s, and continued into the 1970s. Rene Spitz, William Goldfarb, and John Bowlby became interested in the physical and psychological traits of infants housed in institutions. Most of their studies—based on methodologies that were sometimes criticized—predicted negative results for orphaned children. They cited behavior problems, immaturity, and the inability to form relationships.

Later studies prepared by Broussard, DeCarie, and Barbara Tizard suggested that lowering child-caregiver ratios and providing perceptual stimulation in orphanages increased children's intelligence quotient and that effects of deprivation were not irreparable. In the 1990s researchers once again covered the effects of international institutionalism on adoptions of Romanian orphans.

MARIJA PLATACE FUTCHS FINE

Post-Orphanage Behaviors

Based on reports from adoptive parents of Romanian orphans, a group of New York social scientists made some observations about the effect of institutional care on Romanian adoptees.[10] Terms such as *institutional autism* and *attachment disorder* began to appear in the lexicon.

They wanted to study what was in the biology of a wartime orphan that would either overcome or succumb to a whole range of traumas. Those ordeals included the shock of being separated from parents, the forced adjustment to living in an institution, the loss of one's first language, and the ordeal of adjusting to sometimes negative cultural circumstances.

As I reviewed the ways Romanian orphans acted out against (or gave into) these traumas, I wondered how their institutional experience compared to my own. The study pointed out that because Romanian children did not receive supportive mediation from adults, they continued to be traumatized.

Some children were even forced into survival mode because the Romanian orphanages included rigid routine with ongoing uncontrollable changes in the environment so typical for foreign institutions. There was a frequent turnover of caregivers and transfers of children between institutions, both of which created unpredictability in living arrangements, a high degree of instability, and lack of control.

The constant change in caregivers and frequent transfers of children between institutions did not occur in my situation. It's true that close to forty children in our group of nearly three hundred from Rīga and Majori orphanages died from starvation or diseases in the midst of Allied bombardments during our stay in Germany.

But from what I read of our journeys through Germany, the rest of us remained in reasonably good health, and in my case, I actually thrived. Staff provided us with medicines. They made, mended and laundered our clothing. They taught us to read, write, and appreciate Latvian culture. We put on plays in native costume and observed Latvian celebrations such as Name days.

The one aspect of the Romanian orphan study that intrigued me was what the study called post-orphanage behaviors (POB). They were behaviors American parents observed in their adopted Romanian children. Did my parents note these same behaviors in me?

There were ten: poor self-regulation, mixed maturity, self-parenting, learned helplessness, feeling of entitlement, self-soothing and self-stimulating behavior, extreme attention seeking, hypervigilance and proactive aggressive behavior, controlling and avoiding behavior, and indiscriminate friendliness with strangers.

The report did acknowledge that the range of individual differences was very broad. Despite the negative environment they came from in their Romanian institutions, some adoptees could develop social skills and maturity with time and practice.

More than half of the POBs did not ring true to me. But my father, who gave me feedback on my actions, would have nodded on some of the POBs. He said I showed a mild form of aloofness. The chief example of this was that I did not like being cuddled. The social scientists in the New York study said this conduct was a result from a sense of abandonment, deprivation, and neglect of basic emotional needs.

One POB, "indiscriminate friendliness with strangers," did apply in the case of my first meeting with adoptive Aunt Ave and Uncle Carl. In her letter, Ave wrote that it in the first meeting with them, I enjoyed sitting on their laps.

Extreme attention seeking was definitely a characteristic I had. As a child in an orphanage, I found—as did other children—that adult responsiveness was a rare and valuable commodity. I competed for that consideration, sometimes by showing negative behavior. The marble incident was one instance of getting that kind of notice, unwelcome as the punishment clearly was.

Perhaps that competition for adult caring is the reason I have always been comfortable in the company of individuals much older than myself. A longtime friend who was a generation older than I was called me a gerontophile. It comes as no surprise that my husband, Irwin, was twenty-four years older. He used to joke that after my parents adopted me, he adopted me and that I was his "child bride." But what really came as a thunderbolt was learning that my father, Broņislavs, and my husband, Irwin, were born in the same year, 1919.

One other POB that I showed was controlling and avoiding behavior, which I showed at both home and school. My father told me I had a pattern of staging my naughtiness. I would see just how much I could get away with before he punished me.

The very first time I ratcheted up my misbehavior to such an unacceptable level, he felt he had to give me a paddling. I remember that scene to this day. I was standing next to the refrigerator. My mother watched as my father delivered the stinging blows to my bottom.

I deliberately held back the tears as my way of saying, "I'll show you who's in charge!" It had the anticipated effect; my parents stood there in total silence. I knew they were at a loss as to how to proceed.

Within hours I began a new round of misbehaviors, building from small infractions up to larger ones. John and Selma caught on to my game. The paddlings continued, and after each time, I cried.

Only years later did my father tell me how both he and my mother agonized, for several hours, over that first paddling, worried that they had done irreparable harm to me. But when I started misbehaving just hours later as though nothing had happened, they realized my not crying was just one more way of trying to control them, so the paddlings continued.

They noticed another one of my controlling behaviors. I would do the opposite of what they told me to do. They waged their own successful mental warfare by using reverse psychology. They knew how to outmaneuver me by telling me to do just the opposite of what they wanted me to do. They also acted as a unit: two against one. There was no way I could manipulate or outgame them.

I pulled the same naughtiness at school. Teachers sent me to principal Monroe McPheters for acting out. I don't recall ever being punished. He asked me to sit in his office or outside it for a time before sending me back to class. That kind of behavior stopped by the time I entered the third grade.

Perhaps my willingness to do time-out sessions had something to do with knowing that I was going to the father of my fellow student and best friend, Janie McPheters. Looking back on it now, I probably was subconsciously looking for that adult attention. But in this case, it was no longer punitive but actually rewarding.

The elementary school officials probably expected me to grow out of my misbehaving ways, hoping my language and social skills would come in line with my peers. I don't recall sitting outside any principal's office after we moved to Denver, when I entered the third grade.

The one POB that clearly hit home was my hypervigilance and proactive, aggressive behavior. I recall my adoptive parents telling me what my first play date was like. They reported to me that the Ford girls, Susan and Marcia, were shocked to find I played like "a wildcat."

The way I sometimes played with my first dog, Brownie, was downright cruel. I picked up the end of the leash attached to his collar, tossed him up into the air, and swung him round and round several times, then dropped him into a heap onto the lawn in front of our home.

When Brownie died several years later, I felt guilty, thinking I had caused his death. I asked my mother why he died, expecting her to tell me it was from his being thrown about in some violent manner. She said he died from the hardening and blockage of the arteries, which some years later I read often happened in male dogs.

Fish and frogs were next on the list. I enjoyed the sensation of slamming the heads of the fish my father caught against a rock. He had asked me to do that so that they would not continue to flip endlessly.

I did the same bashing routine with frogs when I was about eight years old. I was with my parents in some wild area of Colorado and picked one up, bashing it against a rock several times to make sure it was dead. It gave me such a thrilling sensation that I found a second frog and repeated the process. I never told my parents what I had done, who were yards away, and am relieved that I never did anything like that again.

Looking back on the ease with which I adjusted to schools and friends in that first year in America, I do believe in what some psychologists say that "language is a psychological function that mediates practically all other psychological competencies, such as perception, memory, emotions, cognition, goal-oriented behavior, and motivation."[11] Language acquisition was the single most important

MARIJA PLATACE FUTCHS FINE

factor in my acculturation process. Living in a monolingual household where my parents acted as powerful facilitators sped up that process.

I lost my mother tongue in the first three months of first grade, which I have read is standard for a six-year-old, internationally adopted child. Getting there did involve the intervention of classmates who sometimes translated what I was saying to teachers. But in the second semester, I was in the fast-reading group. I was thoroughly acculturated by the time I entered the second grade, when classmates elected me to the student council.

Latvian Caretakers in America

Our caretakers took measures to ensure that we would assimilate into the American culture, which meant staying out of our way. They were to keep their distance from us whether we were in Australia, Canada, Brazil, or the United States. There were to be no letters, no telephone calls, and no visits.

It didn't always work out that way, according to the Latvian orphan tracker Jānis Riekstiņš. A few caretakers kept in touch by phone or by letter with their former charges. Perhaps that is why Dr. Bergfelde did not write to me directly, even after fourteen years. I think that's why her niece did not give her aunt's name; she only used the initial *V.* It wasn't until I saw her name appear in articles and books a year ago that I learned her first name was Veronica.

I came to know one case where a caretaker wouldn't let go of an orphan that she had cared for. Her adoptive parents named her Ruth Hoyer. She and her parents came to Denver, where we talked about our time in three orphanages.

She told me how she was at the center of a bitter custody battle, which appeared in the newspaper.[12] The caretaker planned to adopt her once they both arrived in America in 1949. She contacted a Lutheran minister in Germany to help her secure two sponsors in Pennsylvania for herself and Ruth. That action went outside the regular channels for adoption, which only the NLC managed. After rumors of her plans reached the NLC staff, a representative took Ruth away from the caretaker when they landed in New York.

After the Hoyers completed the adoption process in January 1950, the caretaker hired a lawyer to gain custody of her former charge. The court proceedings dragged on into 1951, but in the end, Ruth's parents prevailed, leaving everyone in the process pained and saddened.

In the process of preparing my multigenerational study, I read memoirs of nearly two dozen Latvian Americans who became naturalized American citizens at the same time I did. They related their ways of adapting to a new culture, always with the thought of returning to the land of their birth. Several of them did just that in the 1980s when Latvia was still a Soviet state. It was riveting to read how intimidating the surveillance of the authorities was.

As I prepared to return to the land of my birth, I would not have to worry about that kind of scrutiny, since I was returning to a free Latvia. I would, instead, be anxiously awaiting a visit with the one living relative who knew me as an infant, Tante Leonora, and meeting a brother I never knew existed until that summer. The excitement I felt was palpable.

Home Movies
Stills of my adoptive mother and me
from film taken by my adoptive father, John Futchs
Boulder, Colorado May 1949

CHAPTER 15

Return

What Happened to Her Curly Hair?

Rīga

A S THE AIRPLANE eased down onto the tarmac at Rīga International Airport on that summer's day in 2014, I had the oddly pleasant sensation that I belonged there. Outside the airplane window, I viewed red roofs on one-story buildings. I felt a warm happiness, a comfortable, at-home feeling.

Even though I had no reason to expect that I would have flashbacks to my days in Rīga, I still hoped there would be a smell, a song, or a person's face that would trigger a recollection from that time. Revisiting towns from my past was something I enjoyed doing. I liked contrasting the remembered past to the changed present. My school building in Boulder was there, but the creek running next to it was gone. My playground at an elementary school in Denver was there, but the loop rings I used to swing on were gone.

As I scanned the Rīga skyline in the taxi ride to my hotel, the horizon revealed a pleasing range of the old-world buildings alongside the gleaming, modern structures of the radio and TV tower and the spectacular National Library. Dominating the scene was the massive blocklike structure, which Lauris later pointed out was the ex-Science Academy.

I remembered seeing seven similar structures in my visit to Moscow in 1993, all of them examples of the art and architecture of socialist realism. They have inspired a range of names from the prosaic to the fanciful. Russians refer to them as the seven skyscrapers. Tourists call them them the Stalin buidings or Seven Sisters. I prefer Lauris's term for the building in Rīga as "Stalin's birthday cake." However one might wish to describe them, the immensity and impenetrability of those buildings seemed to me to symbolize a system that obstructed the search for my origins for half a century.

After settling into the Radisson BluHotel in the city center, I pulled out my papers for the journey that Lauris had mapped out for Rīga and the Latvian provinces. We met right after breakfast in the lobby.

He came up from behind me in the lobby and announced himself, "Here I am!" He was a tall, youthful, energetic, and fit man dressed in Bermuda shorts and T-shirt, sporting sunglasses. With his short beard and mustache, he reminded me a little of the Mexican actor Gael García Bernal.

After taking a bus across the Daugava River, we went on foot through the residential area where Rīga Orphanage still stands. That fifteen-minute walk through Pārdaugava's Kalnciema Quarter (*Kalnciema kvartāls*) took me back to a world that had not changed since 1944.

Being in a place I had lived in seven decades earlier gave me a sense of exhilaration. As I moved from street corner to street corner, I started taking pictures.

When we came upon the orphanage, I was impressed to learn it was the same building I had been in decades earlier. This fact was to amaze and impress me all through this visit. Buildings I was in so long ago were still standing. As an adult, I could see what I could not possibly remember when I was one year old. It didn't matter that I wouldn't recognize the yard outside the orphanage or that I couldn't recall the steps leading up to the entrance.

One feature about the orphanage struck me. The book staff used to mark physical milestones in children was the same oversize book the caretakers kept in 1944 to track "its little inhabitants."

The director, Lelde Brīvere, took me around the property, showing the rooms where children were playing and laughing. Sunlight filled the clean rooms. Pictures decorated the walls. Toys sprawled out on what looked like two expensive Persian carpets. It was an idyllic scene, unlike the war years, when food was scarce, resources were limited, diseases were rampant, and there was a nervous tension in the air.

Cēsis

Within hours, we were off in Lauris's Volvo to Cēsis, fifty-five miles to the west, to see Aunt Leonora, guardian of the Platacis family lore. On the way, we stopped at a nursery to buy seedlings that I would plant at the graves of my mother and father. The anticipation of seeing the woman who babysat for me the first months of my life gave me a few anxious moments. Lauris and I had talked about this first meeting in our e-mail exchanges, knowing it would be the *one big event* of my return trip.

As we traveled through the countryside, I wondered what Aunt Leonora's reaction would be to me at this reunion. Neither one of us had any way of knowing what the other looked like. We exchanged no pictures in the lead-up to our visit. She spoke no English and had no Internet connection.

From a distance I saw a large Latvian flag waving in the breeze on that cool August day. It stood at the entrance to the long driveway leading up to the country house and its surrounding grounds. As we pulled into the driveway, a small cat scampered across the gravel driveway.

As I got out of the car, Lauris took out his video camera and called out, *"Leonora! Mēs esam šeit!"* ("Leonora, we're here!") A grandmotherly figure with the dignified bearing of a matriarch emerged, cane in hand, with gentle, welcoming smile on her face. The color of her skirt and blouse matched the rich burgundy color of the Latvian flag.

Lauris positioned his videotape, ready to catch the hug and kiss that aunt and niece would give each other. When she enfolded me in her arms, the feeling was unmistakable. I. Was. Home.

Though she had not seen me in seven decades, she recalled one of my physical traits that was missing. Directing her remark to Lauris, she

asked, "Kas noticis ar viņas cirtām?" ("What happened to her curls?")
My fine, wispy hair had lost its natural curl.

Waiting for us inside were her son from her second marriage, Valdis; his wife, Dina; and Leonora's third husband, Jānis Dambītis. Lauris translated as my aunt talked about her two sons, both in their fifties. One is married and lives in Belarus, with whom she exchanges occasional visits. The second son, Valdis, lives in Cēsis and works as a car mechanic. Leonora has three granddaughters and two great-grandchildren.

As we sat around the breakfast table, enjoying the breakfast which Leonora prepared for us, we got the story about her third husband. Jānis, eighty-eight years old, is eight years her senior. Both of them were widowed when they met.

Jānis worked as a farmer and doctor of veterinary medicine, during which time he built his own house and married another doctor. He was one of the thousands of Latvians deported in 1941 to Krasnoyarsk,[1] punished for being a kulak, the independent farmer Soviets replaced with its system of collectivization in 1946.

After Stalin's death in 1961, Soviets allowed Jānis to return from Siberia with his wife and two children. When he and his wife learned that the Soviets barred them from returning to the private home he had built in Ērgļi,[2] they considered returning to Siberia, even knowing how much they had disliked living there. But in the end, they decided to stay, living in the housing Soviets provided its citizens.

Jānis had one of the most ingratiating smiles I have ever seen. His gentle bearing, especially after he had experienced the harsh conditions of the gulag, impressed me. He volunteered to Lauris what he thought of his Leonora, "I take good care of her, and we have a happy life together."

She took me by the hand and led me from room to room in her home, to pictures of grandchildren on shelves, and the crockery and cups placed on lace liners in cabinets. I was charmed at this gesture on her part and took several video clips of the interior.

Then Leonora took out several boxes holding the family photos. There were pictures of my father, grandfather Silvestrs, grandfather Augusts, her wedding photos, and one of the family traitor, Alberts.

I focused in on my father's face. I saw no resemblance, at least not in the face. But there was one similarity—how his hair wound up into a slight tuft. I have a similar crop of hair, not as curly as his, but it juts up in the same way.

There were no pictures of my mother. I took out my photos from age six on up to the present. Leonora reviewed them all and pointed to the one which she felt looked most like my mother; it was a photo of me at age twenty-one.

Andrupene

After breakfast, Leonora loaded up her belongings and food she had prepared for the two-day journey to Andrupene, Rēzekne, Dobele, Jaunpils, and Salaspils, the towns representing the pivotal moments in my early life. They would run the spectrum, from the warm places marking happy, family milestones to the lonely, terrifying prisons.

More important than walking through structures and buildings would be meeting blood relatives who had lived in parallel universes during my time in America. One person was known to me at birth, Leonora. The other was my half-brother Andris.

Leonora prepared well-seasoned pieces of chicken, a loaf of the nutritious sourdough rye bread for which Latvians are famous, and a delicately spiced salad, all of which sustained us for half a dozen meals on the three-day trip. None of it ever spoiled, despite the fact that the food was not kept in a refrigerated box in the car.

Leonora secured the lodging at Dana cabin in Andrupene, right next to a small lake into which Lauris jumped for a quick dip in what had to be a chilling body of water. I cringed as I watch him dive in. The cabin provided the extreme opposite sensation, a sauna on the first floor set at full blast. It heated the entire cabin so much that it went straight up into the attic, curling our toes as we slept.

Visits to family graves in two cemeteries took me back through two generations of my family. Latvian cemeteries are forests that envelop one. The natural setting assumes a larger importance than the tombs in it. They are set deep inside coniferous forests, where the crisp air and gentle breezes carry the subtle scent of the evergreens.

Leonora placed gladiolas into a stand next to her mother Helēna's grave. She held up one stem and, while looking in my direction, said, "Tas viens ir no tevis." ("This one is from you.")

At my mother's grave, I planted one of the two saplings I had bought at the nursery outside Cēsis. Her coworker at the kolkhoz said the cause of her death was "old age." She was sixty-eight years old when she died. Leonora gave the same reason—old age—as the cause of death for several family members. Was it a way to avoid mentioning diseases that had a stigma attached to them?

The reason I asked the question was to determine the family medical history, which could give me some idea what predispositions I might have toward a disease or another. I have been remarkably lucky in that regard, never having been hospitalized my entire life.

What sent chills up and down my spine was seeing the year of death on my mother's grave. It was the same year my adoptive mother died. To think that they shared not just that similarity but also their names, Solomeja and Selma. That was a nice thought. Whether one calls it karma, coincidence, or just a fortunate confluence of events in my life, I liked that connection.

There was one other pleasant surprise, the only gravestone to bear an image of the entombed person, Leonora Danovska, the younger sister of my mother. That excited me no end. Now I had a picture of my mother's nearest kin. I felt I did bear a likeness to her.

People who knew both Solomeja and Leonora described my mother as the more serious of the two. Leonora was "sharp and witty." Leonora's tombstone was the only one to have both a picture and an inscription on it. The message said, "The heart doesn't beat anymore, but it still had a song to sing and the eyes had to shine watching life."

The church and family home in Andrupene came next. Aunt Leonora led us to the church where my parents met in the choir, were married, and where I was christened. It was a simple white wooden church with an imposing name: the Andrupene Roman Catholic Church of the Holy Mother Mary. Such a lofty name might suggest why the priest said Mārīte—suggested by Leonora, meaning "lady bug"—was not an appropriate name for its priest to bestow on a newborn.

Leonora took us to her home, where I lived for a few months before my father finished building our home. The new owners moved it several years ago from Rusiški village to the town of Malta, a few miles down the road. It was a funny coincidence that the house stood on Andrupene Street in Malta.

The current owners, a young couple with two children, welcomed us to take a look around. The sauna where I was born no longer existed; it was in a separate building next to Augusts's home. But I did see the room where my parents probably took me for visits to Grandfather Augusts and Grandmother Helēna. Standing in that room was a singular experience. I tried imagining ten people seventy years earlier, sleeping, eating, and learning to be apprentices in that space.

The room, which seemed small as I stood in it, was made smaller since the current family cut the large room in two, allowing the son and daughter to have their own private spaces. Nuclear families of four or five people have replaced the communal living arrangements suitable for groups of eight and ten persons of seven decades ago.

Rēzekne

The cold, rainy weather in Rēzekne and Ančupāni Hills were appropriate barometers for what both places represented to my family. The prison building is left as a hoary ghost of past Nazi atrocities. It did not merit even being made into a museum.

There were boarded-up windows and doors. Peeling paint on the outside walls looked like someone had streaked their nails against it, anguished at the thought of what went on inside. I moved around the entire building to take in the dimensions of the prison where I spent three months with my mother and grandmother in 1944. The chill in the air is what I felt, not unlike what all of us experienced inside the walls.

Because of the brutalities the prison once housed, it stood in strange juxtaposition to the stately Roman Catholic Church of the Holiest

Jesus Heart directly across the street. From every angle of the prison, the church looms above the concrete building that contained so much suffering. I wonder if the sight or proximity of the church helped my great-uncle, grandmother, and mother to endure their ordeal.

An equally mournful scene was Ančupāni Hills, a few miles outside Rēzekne. Soviets did memorialize it. I watched Leonora as she walked, cane in hand, along the Alley of Suffering. To her right were thousands of tall conifer trees, standing for the eighteen thousand men, women, and children murdered by the Nazis.

A graceful statue of a female figure holding a child in her arms stood next to a sign on a wall with the words "Viņi mira, lai dzīvotu tu" ("They died so you could live"). These were haunting words, marking the place where my grandfather Augusts dropped into the pit that his brother Kazimirs was forced to dig for him before the guards shot him.

Dobele

The visit to Dobele, forty-seven miles from Rīga, brought me face-to-face with my father's second son from his marriage to Antonija. We both eyed each other with a studied gaze. Did we have each other's eyes? Yes. Both were blue.

But where he has a steady, piercing gaze, I do not. Our somatic types were also different. Where he is tall and stout, I am short and slight. His wife, Zinaīda, was an attractive lady sporting a short, stylish bob. She had studied beauty culture and is a retired beautician. Andris continues to work as an agronomist.

Zinaīda ingratiated herself to me by asking me to call her Nida. She also spoke a few words of English, well beyond the half dozen Latvian phrase I know. Immediately, Andris took out photo albums, picking out pictures of our father as I busily took snapshots of them. He had pictures of our father in his later years. That is where I saw that we had similar faces and somatic types.

No sooner had I taken around two dozen photos, labeling each on my Notes on my iPad, when Zinaīda pointed to pictures of their three sons on a nearby counter. They live in Scotland. I now had a new destination—Inverness, Scotland—to see nephews Andris, Jānis, and Arnis.

Going to my father's grave included a drive down a narrow dirt road between rows of trees, which formed a perfect column through which which we passed. Just as I had planted the seedling next to my mother's grave, I dug a hole for the other sapling next to my father's grave. It was a soulful experience, standing next to my half-brother, honoring our father. And how fitting it was. My father searched for me for two decades until I found him four decades later.

In our two visits, Andris related what little he knew about my father and his second wife.[3] Antonija and my father lived apart for most of their married lives. Jānis lived with our father as they were growing up. Andris lived with his mother.

Andris believed our father preferred a secure life to one marked with adventure. The only risk-taking venture he had was his partisan activity in his early twenties. Who knows if that wartime experience, which resulted in the loss of his family, precluded his ever taking such a bold action again?

He was very religious, participating in church activities on a regular basis. He tried to involve his children in the church. Jānis was more into it than Andris, who chose not to be baptized. My brother jokingly refers to himself as a pagan.

Andris remembered our father playing the balalaika, mandolin, and accordion. He continued his passion for carpentry, making barrels and furniture. He made skis for his sons.

He was a nature lover and often went fishing with his brothers Vitālijs and Jāzeps. Broņislavs also worked as a beekeeper, spending a lot of time building hives. He continued these pursuits up until he died of a stroke at age seventy-three.

Broņislavs never spoke of Solomeja in front of his sons. But Andris felt his mother was "slightly annoyed" whenever his father talked about his ex-wife. From time to time, Andris overheard his mother saying to Broņislavs, "There you go again with your Solomeja!"

Andris also recalled that Broņislavs said to both his sons on one occasion, "Do you know you have a sister somewhere in the world?"

MARIJA PLATACE FUTCHS FINE

He would have told them that after 1961, when he learned from the Russian Red Cross that I had been adopted by some unnamed couple somewhere overseas.

Even though my father was a Soviet partisan in his early twenties, he was not a Communist. He was strongly opposed to both occupying powers, particularly the Russians. However, he enjoyed using his privileges as a former decorated Soviet partisan. As one of the more than one thousand Soviet partisans who fought for Latvia in 1941–1944, he was awarded orders, decorations, and medals of the Soviet Union.[4]

That gained him entry into the Occupants' Store, a special shop for war veterans. Before going into the shop, he put on the uniform and war medals. He bought coffee, meat, and other daily goods that were unavailable to most others.

The privileged purchasing powers he had made him the first person in the kolkhoz to own a TV. Andris recalled that whenever he watched figure skating with his dad, Broņislavs always rooted for the Americans or Germans. In fact, he cheered for anyone that was up against the Russians.

My father was no different than his father, and my grandfather Augusts, as far as their hatred for the Russians. Where Augusts placed his faith in Latvia's first president, Kārlis Ulmanis, to rescue Latvians from the Russians in the '40s, Broņislavs put his faith in the Americans to drive the Russians out of Latvia in the '50s. He used to chase his boys out of the room in order to listen to the *Voice of America* on the radio. He hoped that the Americans would liberate Latvia from the Soviets by honoring its commitment to the Atlantic Charter.

However, Andris didn't judge his father's support of the Soviets during the war. He realized that the '40s were difficult times, when maintaining a neutral stance was out of the question. One had to choose sides. In that regard, my father was prescient; he banked on the Germans losing, and they did.

The long-held belief in a free Latvia seems to have taken root during the time my grandfather Augusts became a wealthy kulak. Though a soldier in the Imperial Army as his father was, he believed in a free Latvia. That belief reached down to my father, who was convinced that there would be an independent Latvian state again. That's why it pleased me to know that in his last year, Broņislavs lived once again in an independent Latvia.

Three years after my father died, his brother Vitālijs kept up the search for me. When he read my name in Jānis Riekstiņš' book, *Bāra Bērni*, he sought him out. Jānis, with whom I spoke in a Skype session arranged by Lauris in May 2015, described Vitālijs as a "strong" man who visited him for about a half an hour.

I can believe that Vitalijs had that kind of high profile. He was, according to Leonora, the most educated sibling and rose up through the ranks of the Latvian police force. Jānis recalled very little of that conversation, but it was not about politics. He only mentioned to Vitālijs that the Germans had captured my family and there were no leads he could suggest for him to pursue.

Andris Kairišs

I met with my half-brother's best friend, Modris Samušs, in Andrupene. He described my half-brother both in physical and personal terms. He said Andris could have been my twin.

Modris couldn't tell me anything about Solomeja, since he met Andris after she died, when my brother was twenty-five years old. All he knew from what Andris told him was that his father died when he was three years old and that Solomeja raised him as a single parent.

Andris completed five grades of school, where he made good marks. He took up farming, drove a tractor, and delivered food to people. By every account, he was a kind, gentle person who would do any favor for anyone.

But the downside to his gentle nature was that he had a low self-esteem. He let people walk all over him. He was unlucky at love, having had two failed marriages. His first marriage ended in divorce and no children. His second marriage ended in his death.

A man twenty years younger than Andris came between him and his second wife. Rather than confront the man his wife was intimately involved with, he allowed the relationship to go on under his own roof without doing anything to stop it. It took his wife's action—taking money out of their joint bank account to buy a car for her lover, who totaled it a few days later—for him finally to take action.

But when he finally confronted the younger man, he was ill equipped to do so. He was in a drunken state and no match for the younger man, who threw him to the ground and stomped on his chest, puncturing his lung. To make matters worse, my brother did nothing about his injury, which pained him for days. He ignored the chest pains before asking his friend, Modris, to take him to the hospital for treatment. By then it was too late; he died ten days after the fight.

When I heard about my brother's unfortunate, sad end, I wondered how Solomeja's wartime experience affected her approach to parenting. Might she have been an overprotective mother, unable to teach him to stand up for himself? Did she find herself in compromised situations in the camp that left her unable to fend for herself? Did that experience leave her with a defeatist point of view? Is that why she never taught her son how to stand up to bullies?

The one really curious piece of information Modris related to me was that in his last year, 2010, Andris said he had a half-sister living in America. That astounded me. How did Solomeja's son know my exact location?

I have no evidence that my mother conducted a search for me, as my father did. My parents never spoke to each other after their divorce, so Broņislavs would never have told her what he learned from the search he made with the Russian Red Cross, i.e., that I had been adopted by a couple in some undisclosed country.

So how did she pinpoint my location and pass this information on to her son, when not even my father knew what country I was in? I asked Modris whether Andris took the next step of trying to find me, a question Modris posed to Andris as well. He said Andris shrugged his shoulders, saying he didn't know how to go about doing it.

The more I thought about how improbable Solomeja's statement to Andris was, the more her story about the German kept coming back to me. She had come up with two stories for which she gave no evidence. She knew her German was never coming. But to avoid the scorn and ridicule of villagers, she created the story that she convinced herself to be true.

She might have done the same thing when she told her son that he had a sister in America. There were stories in newspapers and books by Jānis Riekstiņš, among others, stating that American couples had adopted Latvian orphans. It's only speculation on my part, but I think she chose to believe I was one of them. The fact that she had no evidence for that didn't matter. I like to think she wanted to believe I survived.

Salaspils

The visit to Salaspils left a lasting impact on me. Its green lawns and tall trees gave it a peaceful feeling. At the entrance there is a sign on the slate grey wall, "Beyond these walls the earth weeps." Inside is a marble slab from which there comes the continuous recording of a beating heart. The message is powerful. While humiliations and tortures happened there, the human spirit prevailed.

Inside the memorial is a wall depicting startling black-and-white images of what the camp was like. The images show the tower and the gallows, and for me, the truly electrifying scene was of the soldiers separating mothers from their children.

The scene showed the anguish on the mothers' faces and the terror on children's faces as soldiers pulled them apart. That stabbing image is the lasting one I took with me from Salaspils. While it was a "death" camp to many, it was where I lost my mother.

Two Identities Joined

As a WWII orphan and adoptee, I have carried two identities that were closed off from each other until now. Being able to merge them into one was a journey into the self. The trip back to Latvian buildings and places allowed me to experience as an adult what I couldn't comprehend as an infant. The unchanged physical setting enabled me to imagine that early life.

Visualizing past events in the unchanged physical world of my Latvia gave me a faint but distinct echo of those occasions. My journey back in time gave me a feeling of being present in the past. But more than the buildings was the one real and wondrous experience of connecting with the one surviving member of my family, my father's youngest sister. I felt the embrace of my birth family when she and I met, a sensation words still have no power to express. She was the link between the two Marijas. Reuniting with Tante Leonora is the most personally rewarding experience of my life.

Andris Kairišs, ca. 1973
son of Solomeja and Andreijs Kairišs
Photo Courtesy of Lauris Olups

With Aunt Leonora and Brother Andris, Jaunpils 2014
Photo by Lauris Olups

L–R: Andris Platacis, son Andris Lastovskis, Andris's partner,
Sanita Steina, Zinaīda Platace, wife of Andris Platacis
On laps: Keita and Līva Lastovskis 2014

L–R: Nephews Arnis and Jānis Platacis, myself, and
Andris Lastovskis, Aberdeen, Scotland, 2015

Photos by Andris Lastovskis

A Glitch in the Family Legend

T HE LEGEND [1] is that Abrams Platacis was a Jewish grocer living in St. Petersburg, Russia in the nineteenth century who married his maid, a Latvian Christian lady, whose name is unknown. Abrams sired one child, Silvestrs, who served in the Russian Imperial Army and married Dominise/Domicile. Abrams gave money to Silvestrs to purchase land in Latgale, then a part of the Russian Empire. Silvestrs took his family to Rusišku sādža, where they became wealthy kulaks in that region of Russia (now Latvia). Silvestrs's grandson, my father, continued that tradition until March 13, 1944, when the war destroyed the independent farming tradition of the Platacis family.

Some parts of the legend are true, some cannot be proven. No Russian documents exist for Abrams. The first time individual census reports appeared in Russia was 1897.[2] The only documents that mention him or indirectly relate to him are two Latvian documents which strongly suggest that he spent time in Latvia.

Abrams was probably born in Latvia where he secured property, started his family with his wife, the Latvian Christian who was his maid. Though Abrams was Jewish, his child's religion passed down through his mother. That would explain why Silvestrs was Christian, which continued down through the succeeding generations.

The 1935 Census Reports [3] for Abrams's son, Silvestrs, and his wife, Domicile, show that they were born in Rēzekne, Latgale, in 1860 and 1866 respectively. That seems to indicate that Abrams was there at the same time. It is likely that several years after the birth of Silvestrs,

Abrams took his family to St. Petersburg, where Silvestrs joined the Russian Imperial Army.

While serving as a soldier, Silvestrs could have been stationed in Latgale where he met and married Domicile, and started his family. He and his wife could have joined his father Abrams who migrated to St. Petersburg. It is there that Silvestrs and Domicile could have welcomed the arrival of their first born, Augusts, in 1890 in St. Petersburg. No birth record exists for Augusts, but according to legend, he, like his father, joined the Russian Imperial Army.

There are two possible scenarios for how the Platacis clan came to Latvia. The forebears for Abrams could have been from any number of ethnic groups who arrived in Latgale as early as the 16th century. That migration could have started from any number of countries: Poland, Lithuania, Ukraine, or Byelorussia (current day Belarus). After several generations in the Latgale region, where they acquired the name of Platacis, the enterprising Abrams, born perhaps, sometime around 1840, could have decided to take his family of three to Saint Petersburg after his son Silvestrs was born in Latgale in 1860.

Another way the ancestors of Abrams could have entered Latvia was as Russian Jews who were forced to leave Moscow or Saint Petersburg after Czarina Catherine established the Pale of Settlement for Jews in 1791. [4] The Latgale region of Latvia was in the Pale, [5] specifically, in the Vitbesk area. To blend in more successfully into their communities Abrams's Russian forebears might have acquired the Latvian name of Platacis. When Abrams was born in Latgale, he went by two names. One was Latvian - Ignats. The other was Jewish - Abrams. Once the Pale ended in 1918, Jews could settle in Russia, when Abrams left behind Ignats and kept the name of Abrams after he returned to the land of his ancestors.

One Latvian document [6] named Silvestrs as the son of Ignats. It requested ownership of property from Kazimirs and Adeļa, the children of Silvestrs Platacis. Kazimirs signed for himself and for Silvestrs, who could not read or write, whose illiteracy was verified by the 1935 Latvian census.

MARIJA PLATACE FUTCHS FINE

**Request for landownership, which
identifies Ignats (Abrams) as Silvestrs's father**

**Great-Uncle Alberts, Great-Grandfather Silvestrs,
and Grandfather Augusts, ca. 1920
Photo from Leonora Platace's family album**

ACKNOWLEDGMENTS

F RIENDS AND FAMILY members from Latvia, Germany, and America provided invaluable resources on which this narrative is based. College classmate Nancy Peterson prompted me to make the first search for my parents in 1962, which introduced me to Dr. Veronika Bergfelde, the director of my orphanage. That information became an important reference point in the search for my origins.

Ilze Vituma, third secretary of the Latvian Embassy in Washington, DC, found the names of my parents, offered helpful leads in my ongoing search, and presented my official birth certificate, complete with the imprimatur of the Latvian Embassy.

Lauris Olups provided his superior "detective skills" in tracking down family members and tapping a wide range of sources. He translated a variety of papers written in Latvian and Russian. He also established my family tree on the Internet and edited my copy, focusing on Latvian phrases, names, and family events.

Latvian family members offered their recollections by phone or through e-mail. Leonora Platace Ķieģelis drew on her phenomenal memory bank to give me the Platacis family lore. Andris Platacis, son of my father's second marriage, gave important personal details about our father. Zinaīda Platace, Juris Sorokins, and Valdis Ķieģelis provided vivid memories of family members.

Valya Volkovitskya and Marga Schmoll translated Russian and German documents related to my mother. Marga also arranged my visit to Hahnenklee and Clausthal, Germany, where she set up the interviews with people who had knowledge of those towns during World War II.

Several individuals offered helpful readings. They are Barbara Gholz, Margaret Chambers, and Lilita Bergs, who also provided the key contact of the International Tracing Service of UNESCO.

Interviews with persons in the United States and Germany helped to round out the narrative. My telephone interview with Evelyn Hidy provided information about the orphanage experience her adopted children and I shared in Hahnenklee, Germany. Latvian immigrants Maija Stumbris, Ruta Praulina, and Rita Drone gave me a picture of the displaced persons camp they and my mother lived in after the war. Frank Helge, archivist in Clausthal, Germany, gave useful information about wartime Germany in the 1940s. My Skype session with Jānis Riekstiņš—many of whose books and articles formed the backbone of two chapters—afforded me the chance to talk about the visit my Uncle Vitālijs had with him in the 1900s.

The copy editors at Xlibris, Lois Weinberg, Anita Terauds, and Camille Cook provided their outstanding proofreading skills and helpful comments.

Marija Fine is a naturalized American citizen who was adopted by the Reverend John and Selma Futchs. She grew up in Colorado and Texas and graduated from Midland University (Fremont, Nebraska) with a BA in history in 1965. She received an MA from the School of International Studies at the American University in Washington, DC, in 1970. She taught English as a second language as an educational missionary for the Lutheran Church in Malaysia from 1965 to 1968, and she was an instructor at Taiwan Normal University in Taipei from 1973 to 1974. As an educator in Washington, DC, she was a school administrator at Bell Multicultural High School, consultant to the US Department of Education, information specialist at the National Education Association, and computer professional at WAVE, Inc. Her husband, Irwin Fine, whom she married in 1978, died of Alzheimer's disease in 2011.

Nazi soldiers seized the baby Marija and her mother, Solomeja, on March 13, 1944, as reprisal for the father Broņislavs Platačs's partisan activities in Latgale, Latvia. Soldiers took mother and child as political prisoners to Rezekne Prison and Salaspils concentration camp. Solomeja was sent to German concentration camps; Marija was taken to orphanages in Latvia and Germany. In 1949 Marija was flown to America, adopted by American parents, and became a US citizen. For seventy years, her origins were unknown to her due to the Soviet occupation of her native Latvia. A family detective in Riga unlocked the story about her parents in 2014, enabling Marija to be reunited with the one surviving member of her father's family, Broņislavs's sister Leonora. The discovery process opened Marija's eyes to her identity, true to her family name Platačs, which means "wide eyes."

NOTES

Chapter 1: The Arrests

[1] Latvian Police Battalions were World War II paramilitary units created from Latvian volunteers and conscripts by the Nazi German authorities who occupied the country from June 1941 to June 1944. Police battalions carried out guard duties and raids against Soviet partisans and fought on the Eastern Front. Wikipedia, "Latvian Police Battalions," last modified on December 13, 2015, http://en.wikipedia.org/wiki/Latvian_Police_Battalions.

[2] Latvian term for "Russian village" (*Rusišku* for "Russian" and *sādža* for "village or hamlet"), http://Imtranslator.net/Latvian to English Translation.

The village dates back to the seventeenth century, after the Old Believers' villages or Old Ritualists, separated from the official Russian Orthodox Church as a protest against church reforms introduced by Patriarch Nikon of Moscow between 1652 and 1666. In Latgale there are Russians, Polish, Russians, Belarusians, and Latvians. Augustnas Žemaitis, "Old Believer," www.onlatvia.com/Old-Believer. (accessed January 5, 2016)

[3] Leonora Platace Ķieģelis, taped audio interview, Andrupene, Latvia, August 2014 (family lore).

[4] The Latvian Legion was created in January 1943 on the orders of Adolf Hitler following a request by Reichsführer-SS Heinrich Himmler. The first members came from Latvian Schutzmannschaft auxiliary police battalions. One month after its founding, German

occupation authorities in Latvia started conscripting military-age men. Those trying to avoid conscription were arrested and sent to concentration camps. Only fifteen to twenty percent of the soldiers serving in the legion were actual volunteers. Wikipedia, "Latvian Legion," last modified February 28, 2016, en.wikipedia.org/Latvian Legion.

5   A kulak was a wealthy landowning farmer, a peasant in Russia wealthy enough to own a farm and hire labor. The word *kulak* originally referred to independent farmers in the Russian Empire who emerged from the peasantry and became wealthy following the Stolypin reform, which began in 1906. Wikipedia, "Kulak," last modified February 28, 2016, "http://en.wikipedia.org/Kulak.

6   Lea Winerman, "Why we can't remember when . . . The hippocampus's role in memory may help explain why we cannot remember our early childhood, and why stress affects our memory later in life," *American Psychological Association* 36, no. 10, http://apa.org/Why we can't remember when... November 2005. (accessed December 13, 2015)

Chapter 2: The Platacis Family

1   The following narrative is based on Leonora's family lore, drawn from conversations with her in 2015.

2   The *daina* is the root of Latvian and Lithuanian poetry dating back to the tenth century. A daina documents the Latvian respect for nature, family, and a strong work ethic. The cycle of life, birth-marriage-death (including the associated rituals), is a common thread. Wikipedia, "Latvia; Daina," www.poetrymagnumopus. com/Latvia:Daina (accessed January 10, 2016)

3   Eiženija Reitmane, "Latviešu Tautas Dziesmas/Latvian Dainas/ Daina 3404, *Heavenly Wedding*, www.latviandainas.lib.virginia. edu/Latviešu Tautas Dziesmas (Latvian Dainas). (accessed December 12, 2015)

4   Kārlis Ulmanis was a prominent Latvian politician during Latvia's independence from 1918 to 1941. He was particularly popular with the farming community because of his focus on agricultural

concerns. He earned a bachelor of science degree in agriculture from the University of Nebraska–Lincoln, a degree he earned in a period when he was in exile, after the 1905 Revolution. Wikipedia, "Kārlis Ulmanis," last modified February 3, 2016, http://en.wikipedia.org/Kārlis Unmanis.

5   Silvestrs Platacis purchased property in Latgale during the Russian Empire. When it collapsed in 1917, legal and banking systems collapsed with it. There are two landownership documents showing the property Silvestrs and three of his four sons owned. The first, dated June 28, 1929, is titled *Andrupenes Pagasts, Rusiški* (Andrupene Parish, Rusiški). It provides the host list, with family name followed by given name. It gives a different spelling of Silvestrs (Platačs Selivestrs). It also provides the land area he owned in hectares, 15.61 (*Lemes platiba ha, 15,61*).

The second document is a handwritten paper dated July 16, 1929, titled *Gemes Terīcības Vistneša N 333* (Land Survey Journal N 333), signed by P. Ozalins [sp?], who vouched for the correctness of the statement (*Par irsansta pareizibu mērmieus*). The report shows that Kazimirs Platacis owned 2.610 hectares (*Platačs Kazimirs 2.610*).

6   *Latvijas Kareivis*, 02.06.1928 [Latvian Soldier, June 2, 1928] in a subsection named "Homeland Chronicles;" **Iekšlietu** *Ministrijas Vēstnesis*, 05.06.1928 [Interior Ministry's Herald, June 5, 1928]; *Daugavas Vārds*, 09.06.1928 [Word of Daugava, June 9, 1928]. All these newspapers are now out of print. The last one was a local Daugavpils newspaper; the other two were published in Riga and had a wide circulation.

7   Ibid.

8   The monetary unit, *lats*, was first introduced in 1922, replacing the Latvian rubles at a rate of one *lats* to fifty *rubļi*. In 1940, when the USSR occupied Latvia, it replaced the *lats* with the Soviet ruble at par. Lats (plural: *lati* [2–9], *latu* [10 and more]) was the currency of Latvia until it was replaced by the euro on January 1, 2014. Wikipedia, "Latvian Lats," last modified November 25, 2015, http://en.wikipedia.org.Latvian_lats.

Chapter 3: The Partisans

[1]   Livonia is a historic region along the eastern shores of the Baltic Sea. Its origins date back to the twelfth century, when it was an area of economic and political expansion by Danes and Germans. Sweden took over much of the same area after the 1626–1629 Polish-Swedish War. The Russian Empire conquered Swedish Livonia during the course of the Great Northern War. In independent Latvia, between the World Wars, southern Livonia became an administrative region under the traditional Latvian name Vidzeme. Wikipedia, "Livonia," last modified December 30, 2015, http://en.wikipedia.org/Livonia.

[2]   The gulag (acronym for *Glavnoye upravlrniye lagerey*) stands for "Main Camp Administration." It was the Russian government agency overseeing the forced Soviet labor camps in the Stalin era (1930s–1950s). Around thirty thousand such camps were scattered throughout the country. Wikipedia, "Gulag," last modified February 27, 2016, http://en.wikipedia.org/Gulag.

[3]   On June 14, 1941, Soviets rounded up approximately 15,000 persons for exile, including men, women, and children from farming families; they also took landowners, and merchants. S. A. and P. Vecrumba, "Siberian Exile, Life in 'Resettlement' Camps and the GULAG," http://www.latvians.com, Siberian Exile. (accessed September 4, 2015)

[4]   Occupation Museum Foundation, "The Perfidious Agreement," *The Three Occupations of Latvia 1940–1991: Soviet and Nazi Takeovers and the Consequences*, (Riga: 2005), 11, http://www.mfa.gov.lv. (accessed October 4, 2015)

[5]   To replace the German soldiers lost at the Battle of Stalingrad (August 1942–February 1943), Adolf Hitler established, at the request of Reichsfuhrer-SS Heinrich Himmler, the Volunteer Waffen SS Legion in January 1943. Latvian men born between 1919 and 1923 had a choice to join the legion or be sent to a German concentration camp. Since so few volunteered, occupation authorities expanded the range of eligible men to all those born between 1906 and 1928. Still, only fifteen percent to twenty percent

of the Latvian soldiers in the Waffen SS Legion were volunteers. Wikipedia, "Latvian Legion," last modified February 28, 2015, http://en.wikipedia.org/Latvian Legion.

"Volunteering" became a cover for illegal conscription to avoid coming into direct conflict with the 1907 Hague Convention. The dispute over the role and importance of two divisions of Waffen SS has been and still is a divisive factor in Latvian society. A total of 140,000 people were called up to form the Latvian Legion, and about 50,000 of them died in the war or deportations following the restoration of Soviet rule in Latvia. "The Latvian Legion," last modified February 28, 2016, http://www.globalsecurity.org/The Latvian Legion.

6   *Iekšlietu Ministrijas Vēstnesis* [Interior Ministry's Herald], 1930.05.09 [September 5, 1930].

7   John A. Armstrong, ed., *Soviet Partisans in World War II* (Madison, Wisconsin: University of Wisconsin Press, 1964), 276.

8   "Eastern Front/22nd June 1944," Operation Bagration, http://WW2history.com. (accessed December 3, 2015).

9   John A. Armstrong, Ibid., 288.

10   "Major Operations," *Soviet Partisans*, http://www.us.wow.com/Soviet Partisans. (accessed January 14, 2016)

11   "The Partisan Warfare," *Soviet Partisans in Latvia*, last modified January 26, 2016, Wikipedia, http://en.wikipedia.org/Soviet Partisans of Latvia.

Latvian historian Zunda challenged the claim by Aleksandrs Drīzulis that at the end of the war in Latvia there were altogether 20,000 armed partisans and members of the Communist resistance. Antonijās Zunda, "Resistance against Nazi German Occupation in Latvia: Positions in Historical Literature," (Riga, Institute of the History of Latvia, 2005), 150. Valters (ed), *The Hidden and Forbidden History of Latvia*, http://www.president.lv. (accessed October 28, 2015)

12   John A. Armstrong, Ibid. 57.

13   Ibid. 322.

14   "Fašistiskajiem slepkavām-bargu sodu!" [Harsh Punishment to Fascist Murderers], *Padomju Jaunatne* [Soviet Youth], no. 213 (October 29, 1965).

15   Wikipedia, "Estonia, Latvia, and Lithuania, http://en.wikipedia.org/wiki/Soviet_partisans_in_Latvia.

Chapter 4: Rēzekne Prison

1   "Rēzekne History," *Rēzekne*, last modified November 9, 2015, Wikipedia, http://en.wikipedia.org/Rēzekne.

2   Jeff Ansell, "War Criminals in Canada: The issue that won't go away," *The Toronto Star*, August 28, 1982.

3   United States Department of Justice, Federal Bureau of Investigation, "Confidential/ Boļeslavs Maikovskis," http://foia.cia.gov, 1, 15–16.

4   Vince Hunt, "The Forests Hide Deep Secrets…Ancupani," accessed October 20, 2015, http://www.fourstringsgood.blogspot.com/ Ancupani Hills, April 19, 2012.

5   United States Department of Justice, Federal Bureau of Investigation, ibid., 12.

6   Ibid.

7   Modris Eksteins, *Walking since Daybreak: A Story of Eastern Europe, World War II, and the Heart of Our Century*, Kindle ed., Kindle locations 2619–2621 (Boston: Houghton Mifflin Harcourt, 2012).

8   Tara Zahra, *The Lost Children: Reconstructing Europe's Families after World War II*, Kindle ed., Kindle locations 1264–1266 (Cambridge, Massachusetts, and London, England: Harvard University Press, 2011).

Chapter 5: Salaspils

1   The original purpose of the camp during its existence from 1941 to 1944 was a place for exterminating Jews, Romas, communist commissars (officers), and Soviet partisans. Over the years, it became a mixed-use camp. It was a general police prison, later a security police prisoner camp, and finally a forced labor camp. By

the end of 1942, the camp held mainly political prisoners, initially housing individuals brought in from Rīga's central prison, and later politically suspect foreigners, Jews, Romas, mental "defectives," and homosexuals. Wikipedia, "Camp Construction and Changes of Plan," *Salaspils Concentration Camp*, last modified September 6, 2015, http://en.wikipedia.org.Salaspils Concentration Camp.

2   Kalējs was a company commander and first lieutenant of the Latvian Auxiliary Security Police, also known as Arajs Kommando, one of the more well-known killing units during the Holocaust. He ordered one hundred men to murder 28,400 people, ninety percent of them Jews. Wikipedia, "Activities Under Nazi Regime," *Konrāds Kalējs,* last modified March 3, 2016, http://en.wikipedia.org/Konrāds Kalējs.

3   Wikipedia, "Kidnapping of non-Germanic European Children by Nazi Germany," last modified February 15, 2015, http://en.wikipedia.org/Kidnapping of Children by Nazi Germany.

4   Name tags were hung around the necks of children taken from their parents in the Salaspils concentration camp. "Salaspils Concentration Camp," *Russians of Latvia*, http://www.russkije.lv.(accessed December 5, 2015)

5   Grace H. Christ et. al, "Bereavement Experiences after the Death of a Child," *Appendix E, The Parent Role and Loss of a Child,* 553, *http://*www.nap.edu/html/children_die. (accessed November 13, 2015)

6   Robyn Gobbel, "Trauma Doesn't Tell Time-LIVE," May 12, 2014, http://www.gobbelcounseling.wordpress.com/trauma-doesn't-tell-time. (accessed November 14, 2015)

7   Grace H. Christ et al, Ibid. 556.

8   The other, smaller, part of Lebensborn was choosing "racially pure" women to bear children with SS officers and other Nazi officials. Over eighty percent of these women were single, who carried their babies in secret. They gave up their babies for adoption without the public ridicule or shame that would otherwise have been part of such illicit unions. Eight thousand children were born in Germany and became property of the Nazi state, which handled

their education and adoption. The program went beyond Germany into Norway, two in Austria, and one each in Belgium, Holland, France, Luxembourg, and Denmark. "Lebensborn Program PT II: Nazi Kidnapping of Children," *Family Court Injustice,* posted March 4, 2015, http://www.familycourtinjustice.wordpress.com/ Conditions of Transfer.

9   Heinrich Himmler was the second-most powerful man in Germany during World War II. He presided over the security of the Nazi empire and was the key and senior Nazi official responsible for conceiving and overseeing implementation of the Final Solution, the Nazi plan to murder the Jews of Europe. Wikipedia, "Germanization," *Heinrich Himmler,* last modified February 25, 2016, http://en.wikipedia.org/Heinrich Himmler.

10   Historian Tara Zahra writes that the Polish government declared two hundred thousand Polish children fell victim to germanization. Based on a survey of postwar documentation, it has been more credibly estimated that around twenty thousand children were kidnapped from Poland and up to fifty thousand from all of Europe. Figures depend both on the definition of *kidnapping* and the definition of *germanization* in a context in which national loyalties were ambiguous. Many East Europeans voluntarily joined the Nazi Volksgemeinschaft, or the people's community, which appealed to the idea of breaking down elitism and uniting people across divides to achieve a national purpose. Some abandoned their children to German families under material or ideological pressure. Tara Zahra, *The Lost Children,* Kindle ed., [Kindle locations 1797–1801].

11   No figures exist for the number of Latvians taken by Nazis to become forced laborers in their camps. Germans abducted approximately 12 million people from almost twenty European countries; about two-thirds of whom came from Eastern Europe, a total of 4,208,000, or 65.2 percent of the overall total of persons who performed manual labor in the camps. Few machines existed then, requiring inmates to perform manual labor such as shoveling and material handling. The rule demanded that the inmates of German camps be forced to work for the war industry with only basic tools

and minimal food rations until totally exhausted. The need for slave labor grew to a point where even children were kidnapped to work in the operation, called the Heu-Aktion [Hay Action]. Wikipedia, "Forced Workers," *Forced Labour Under German Rule During World War II*, last modified February 24, 2016, http://en.wikipedia.org/ wiki/Forced_labor_under_German_rule).

[12] Wikipedia, "Signs and Symptoms," *Typhoid Fever*, last modified March 2, 2016, http://en.wikipedia.org/typhoid fever.

[13] "Children of Salaspils," Salaspils Concentration Camp, http:// military.wikia.com/Salaspils concentration camp. (accessed December 12, 2015)

Chapter 6: Concentration Camps

[1] Concentration camps were in Austria, Belgium, Czechlosovakia, Estonia, Finland, France, Germany, Holland, Italy, Latvia, Lithuania, Norway, Poland, Russia, and Yugoslavia. There were single-use camps for reprisal killings and extermination. Examples of the latter were camps where inmates were killed on arrival: Auschwitz, Belzec, Chelmno, Majdanek, Sobibor, and Treblinka. Some camps were designed just for rehabilitation and reeducation of the intelligentsia of ethnic Poles. There were also camps holding American officers in POW camps at Konigsberg and Berga. Stutthof served several purposes: filtration, labor, and extermination. A year before my mother arrived, Germans built a crematorium and gas chamber ready to start mass executions. Mobile gas wagons were also on site to achieve the goal of executing 150 people per execution. Jewish Virtual Library, "Concentration Camps: What are Concentration Camps?" http://www.Jewishvirtuallibrary.org. (accessed November 11, 2015)

[2] Chris Webb, "Zbigniew Raczkiewicz Recalled What the SS Officer Said to New Arrivals," Stutthof Concentration Camp, http: // www.holocaustresearchproject.org/Stutthof Concentration Camp. (accessed October 19, 2015)

3   "Total Overview," *Anne Frank*, http://www.annefrank.org. (accessed November 19, 2015)

4   Wikipedia, "Evacuation and Liberation," *Klooga Concentration Camp*, last modified December 5, 2015, http://en.wikipedia.org/klooga_concentration_camp.

5   International Tracing Service, UNESCO, Bad Arolsen, August 27, 2015, *Information concerning this individual's path of persecution during the National Socialist (NS) era*. As a result of the Second World War, the fate of millions of people needed, and still need, to be investigated. As early as 1943, a department was set up within the British Red Cross, on the initiative of Allied Forces HQ, to begin the work of tracing people. "Documentation of the Path of Persecution," *ITS*, http://www.its-arolsen.org. (accessed November 11, 2015)

6   NKVD Latvijas Valsts Arhivs, no. 1821, case no. 20935, released April 1957, Plataća Salomeija Ivana ni 1920 .g *Parbaudes-filtrācijas lieta* (Inspections-filtrations case). NKVD screening and filtration camps were camps originally set up to screen Soviet soldiers from enemy imprisonment or encirclement. Thousands of civilians whom Germans imprisoned required checking as well, including Ostarbeiter (eastern workers), war refugees, and others who returned home after being set free from their camps. The Soviet power considered among its citizens also those living in the Baltic countries, occupied in 1939–1940. "NKVD Filtration Camp,"NKVD Screening and Filtration Camps," *NKVD Filtration Camp*, last modified August 27, 2015, http://en.wikipedia.org/NKVD filtration camp.

7   Chris Webb. Ibid.

8   Ibid.

9   English scientist Francis Galton coined the term *eugenics*, meaning "good birth." It was further developed by Austrian botanist Gregor Mendel's theory that the biological makeup of organisms was determined by certain "factors" that were later identified with genes. Reform-minded proponents of eugenics worldwide offered biological solutions to social problems common to societies experiencing urbanization and industrialization. Observation,

family genealogies, physical measurements, and intelligence tests rank groupings from superior to inferior. Holocaust Encyclopedia, "Science as Salvation: Weimar Eugencies, 1919-1933," last updated January 29, 2016, http://www.ushmm.org/Science as Salvation: Weimar Eugenics, 1919-1933.

10 Neuengamme was established in 1938 as a sub camp of Sachsenhausen concentration camp. It was located on the banks of the Dove-Elbe, a tributary of the Elbe River in the Hamburg suburb in northern Germany. Prisoners had inadequate food, shelter, and medicine. Camp authorities used them for forced labor in camp construction, in the brickworks factory, in river-regulation projects, and on construction of a canal. In all, the SS imprisoned about 104,000 to 106,000 people. The largest nationality were Soviets (34,350). At the end of 1944, there were 37,000–39,000 prisoners in the sub camps; almost 10,000 were women, which included my mother. Holocaust Encyclopedia, "Neuengamme," last modified December 27, 2015, http://www.ushmm.org/Neuengamme.

11 Holocaust Encyclopedia, "Children During the Holocaust, last updated January 29, 2016, http://www.ushmm.org/Children During the Holocaust.

12 Helen Burchell, Cambridgeshire, "Holocaust: The Miracle Babies of KZ Mauthausen-Gusen," last updated January 28, 2015, http://www.news.bbc.co.uk/Holocaust: The miracle babies of KZ Mauthausen-Gusen.

13 Wikipedia, "Concentration Camp," Bergen-Belsen Concentration Camp, last modified November 21, 2015, http://en.wikipedia.org/Bergen-Belsen concentration camp.

14 Kapo is derived from the Italian *capo*, meaning "boss," who was a Nazi concentration camp prisoner given privileges in return for carrying out orders of the SS to maintain control over prisoners. A kapo was often a common criminal and was frequently quite brutal to fellow inmates. Jewish Virtual Library, Concentration Camps: Kapos, http://www.jewishvirtuallibrary.org. (accessed November 4, 2015)

15 Johanna Micaela Jacobsen, "Women's Sexuality in WWII Concentration Camps: Tool for Survival . . . Tool for Oppression," http://www.vho.org/aaargh/fran/actu (accessed November 11, 2015)

16 Ben Shephard, *After Daybreak: The Liberation of Bergen-Belsen, 1945* (New York: Shocken Books, 2005), 82, 145.

17 Email exchanges with Juris Sorokins from February 17-23, 2016.

18 Sępopol was established as one of the five Stutthof sub camps. At its opening, it had nine hundred women and one hundred men."Sub-camp of KL Stutthof in Sepopol-Sites," *Virtual Shtetl*, http://sztel.org.pl/sub-camp-of-kl-stutthof-in-sepopol. (accessed October 18, 2015)

19 Wikipedia, "Ravensbrück Prisoners," Ravensbrück, last modified February 15, 2016, http://en.wikipedia.org/Ravensbrück.

20 Louise Adler, "Female Holocaust Survivors Retell Stories from Ravensbruck camp," *The Australian*, February 16, 2016, http://theaustralian.com.au/ Female Holocaust Survivors Retell Stories from Ravensbruck camp, February 13, 2016.

21 "Morning Roll Call … Evening Roll Call, *Just a Normal Day in the Camps,* http://jewishgen.org. (accessed February 18, 2016)

22 Ancestry, "Irma Grese," *Female Guards in Nazi Concentration Camps*, http://www.Fold 3.com/Female Guards in Nazi Concentration Camps/Ravensbrück. (accessed February 18, 2015)

23 Judith Simons, "I saw the horrors of Nazi concentration camp for women at Ravensbruck," *Express*, January 27, 2015, http://www.express.co.uk. (accessed December 8, 2015)

24 Holocaust Encyclopedia, "Dora-Mittelbau," last updated January 29, 2016, http://www.ushmm.org.

Chapter 7: Rīga Orphanage

1 http://www.vsacriga.gov.lv/ Valsts Sociālās Aprūpes Centrs Rīga [The National Social Care Centre "Riga."], "Par Mums/Vēsture" [About Us/History], informācija atjaunota 04-03-2016 [last update March 4, 2016].

2   Arhiva Kopija, 3072, Platacs Marija gads 1944 2 septembri [The State Social Care Center, Riga Branch—orphanage record, Marija Platacs, September 2, 1944].

3   Gitta Sereny, "Stolen Children: Interview with Gitta Sereny," *Talk*, November 1999, http://jewishvirtuallibrary.org. (accessed November 10, 2015)

4   Jānis Riekstiņš, "Bāreni vacija," *Free Latvia* (1991), "Latvian Orphans in Germany: A Call for an Open Conversation."

5   Dace Darzins, letter, December 6, 1963.

Chapter 8: Swinemunde

1   Because Riga Orphanage was unable to handle the rising number of births along with its fluctuating infant mortality rate (fourteen to nineteen percent), Latvia's People's Welfare Ministry created the Majori National Children's Home in Jūrmala, a seaside town sixteen miles from Rīga. http://www.vsacriga.gov.lv/ Valsts Sociālās Aprūpes Centrs Rīga, Par Mums/Vēsture, informācija atjaunota 04-03-2016 [The National Social Care Centre Riga, About Us/History, last update March 4, 2016].

2   The following account of what happened in the journey from Rīga to Swinemunde comes from Alma Seķe's narrative as it appeared in Jānis Riekstiņš's book, "Latvijas bareni Vacija 1944–1949" [Orphans from Latvia in Germany], *Okupacijas Varu Nodaritie Postijumi Latvia 1940–1990* [The Damages of Post War Occupation of Latvia], Memento Daugavas Vanagi (Stockholm, Toronto, 2000), 215–231.

3   Bangerskis was a Latvian officer who served as minister of war in 1925, when Latvia was an independent country. After he retired in 1936, the general collaborated with the Germans, which positioned him in 1943 to become inspector general of the Latvian Legion. Latvians regard him as one who helped and defended Latvians in difficult moments. Wikipedia, "Biography," *Rüdolf Bangerskis*, last modified January 22, 2016, http://en.wikipedia.org/Rüdolf Bangerskis.

4   Wikipedia, "History," Świnoujśie, last modified February 21, 2016, http://en.wikipedia.org/Swinemunde-Swinoujście.

5   "A Background of Pomerania,"*The Bombing of Swinemunde* (Swinoujście), www.revisionist.net/Swinemunde (Swinoujście), (accessed November 8, 2015). "The Swinemunde Mission 12 March 1945," *Library Shelf Six*, http://www.the467tharchive.org/ Swinemunde. (accessed November 18, 2015)

6   One hundred Reichmarks was roughly equivalent to $420 during WWII. According to http://www.dollartimes.com, 1RM equaled US$4.2 at that time. In 2015 dollars, 1RM equals $68.5. So 100RM in today's currency would be equal to $6,850. Wikipedia, "World War II," *Reichsmark*, last modified February 2, 2016, http:// en.wikipedia.org/Reichsmark.

7   Janis Riekstiņš, *Latvijas Bareni, kuri pazaudeja savu dzimteni* [Latvian Orphans Who are in Your Homeland] (Riga: Mansards, 2015), 63–85.

8   *Leiter*, German for "leader," was a term used by Nazis. A *Gauleiter* was the second-highest Nazi Party paramilitary rank, subordinate only to the higher rank Reichsleiter and to the position of Führer. Wikipedia,"Nazi Germany," *Gauleiter*, last modified November 22, 2015, http://en.wikipedia.org/Gauleiter.

9   http://www.the467tharchive.org/swinemunde. Ibid.

10 "Top Ten Most Destructive Bombing Campaigns in WW II," *War History Online*, http://warhistoryonline.com. (accessed October 12, 2015) and Herbert Weber, "The Swinemunde 1945-Boca Raton 2006-Story," http:www.worldwar2collection.com. (accessed October 20, 2015)

11 The Harz is the highest mountain range in Northern Germany; its rugged terrain extends across parts of Lower Saxony, Saxony-Anhalt, and Thuringia area of Germany. Wikipedia, "Location and Extent," *Harz*, last modified February 29, 2016, http://en.wikipedia.org/ Harz.

12 Janis Riekstiņš, *Latvijas Bareni,* Ibid.

13 Wikipedia, "Rescue of the Danish Jews," last modified February 25, 2016, http://en.wikipedia.org/Rescue of the Danish Jews.

Chapter 9: Hahnenklee

1 Frank Helge (Archivist, Clausthal), interview, Clausthal, Germany, May 9, 2015.

2 "Heimastube, Die Jahre 1941 bis 1950," [The Years from 1941 to 1950], http://www.harzclub-hahnenklee.de/Hahnenklee. (accessed October 30, 2015)

3 Jānis Riekstiņš, *Latvijas Bāreni, kuri pazaudeja savu dzimteni* [Latvian Orphans Who are in Your Homeland] (Riga: Mansards, 2015), 104.

4 Jānis Riekstiņš, "Bāreni vacija" [Orphans in Germany], *Free Latvia*, 1991.

5 Jānis Riekstiņš, "Latvijas bareni Vacija 1944–1949" [Latvian Orphans in Germany 1944-1949]," *Okupacijas Varu Nodaritie Postijumi Latvia 1940–1990* [The Damages of Post War Occupation of Latvia], (Stockholm-Toronto: Memento*Daugavas Vanagi, 2000), 215–231.

6 Jānis Riekstiņš, "Latvijas Bāreni vacija," Ibid.

7 Ibid.

8 "Height Weight Chart/Babies-to-Teenagers," *Height Weight Charts*, http://www.heightweightchart.org. (accessed November 4, 2015)

9 While most of Latvia is historically Lutheran, Latgale is predominantly Roman Catholic, due mostly to Polish influence. Wikipedia, "Religion in Latvia," last modified, November 18, 2015, http://en.wikipedia.org/Religion in Latvia.

10 Advameg, Inc., "History," How Products are Made," accessed October 13, 2015, http://www.madehow.com/marbles.

11 Evelyn Hidy, Telephone interview, June 3, 2015.

12 At the Potsdam Conference, Roosevelt, Churchill, and Stalin met to decide how to administer punishment to the defeated Nazi Germany, which had agreed to unconditional surrender nine weeks earlier, on May 8 (V-E Day). The goals of the conference also included the establishment of postwar order, peace treaty issues, and countering the effects of the war. Wikipedia, "Agreements Made

Between the leaders at Postdam," *Potsdam Conference*, last modified February 16, 2016, http://en.wikipedia.org/Potsdam Conference.

13 Pēteris Aigars (a.k.a. Herberts Tērmanis), *Latviešu Ziņas,* [Latvian News] Nr.68 on September 4, 1948, "Orphans of Latvia's future: Visiting the White House in the Green Harz Hills."

14 A boyar is a derogative for communists, a member of the highest rank of the feudal Bulgarian, Moscovian, Kievan Russian, Wallachian, and Moldavian aristocracies. Wikipedia, "Boyar," last modified March 2, 2016, http://en.wikipedia.org/Boyar.

Chapter 10: Postwar Adjustments

1 The Forest Brothers were Estonian, Latvian, and Lithuanian partisans who waged a guerrilla war against Soviet rule during the Soviet invasion and occupation of the three Baltic states during, and after, World War II. Wikipedia, "In Latvia," *Forest Brothers*, last modified January 29, 2016, http://en.wikipedia.org/wiki/Forest_Brothers).

2 The victory date is when Colonel General Carl Hilpert, Latvia's last army commander, surrendered to Marshal Leonid Govorov. Wikipedia,"Carl Hilpert," last modified January 31, 2016, http://en.wikipedia.org/Carl Hilpert.

3 Latgalian is a Baltic language spoken by 150,000–200,000 people mainly in eastern Latvia, and also in Selonia and Vidzeme. There are also Latgalian speakers in Siberia and Bashkiriya in the Russian Federation. Latgalian is officially considered a variant of Latvian and is protected by the Latvian Language Law. Linguists are divided over the status of Latgalian. Some consider it a dialect; others view it as a separate language. Omniglot, the online encyclopedia of writing systems and languages, "Latgalian (latgalīšu volūda)," http:/www.omniglot.com. (accessed January 10, 2016)

4 A kolkhoz is a Russian collective farm. It comes from Russian, short for *kollektivnoe khozyaistvo.* Wikipedia, "Kolkhoz," last modified October 5, 2011, http://en.wikipedia.org/Kolkhoz.

MARIJA PLATACE FUTCHS FINE

5   About two hundred thousand Balts, not including those living privately in Germany, the Netherlands, Belgium, France, Switzerland, and Italy, had fled. Displaced Latvians started trickling into the DP camps in the spring of 1945. S.A. and P. Vecrumba, "Fleeing the Second Soviet Occupation," Displaced Persons Camps, http://www.latvians.com. (accessed November 17, 2015)

6   Gippsland Multicultural Services, "Post World War 2: Displaced Persons Camps in Europe," June 29, 2011, http://www. culturaldiversity.com.au. (accessed October 11, 2015)

7   Tara Zahra, *The Lost Children: Reconstructing Europe's Families after World War II*, (Cambridge: Harvard University, 2011), Kindle ed., Kindle locations 1575–1578.

8   Ben Shephard, *After Daybreak: The Liberation of Bergen-Belsen, 1945* (New York: Schocken Books, 2005), 131.

9   The Atlantic Charter defined the Allied goals for the postwar world. It stated the ideal goals of the war: no territorial aggrandizement, no territorial changes made against the wishes of the people, self-determination, restoration of self-government to those deprived of it. Wikipedia, "Content and Analysis," Atlantic Charter, last modified March 2, 2016, http://en.wikipedia.org/Atlantic Charter.

10 Rita Drone, Maija Stumbris, and Ruta Praulina, Interview, March 2, 2015, Minneapolis, Minnesota.

Chapter 11: The Divorce

1   NKVD Latvijas Valsts Arhivs, no. 1821, case no. 20935, released April 1957, Plataća Salomeija Ivana ni 1920 .g Parbaudes-filtrācijas lieta (Inspections-filtrations case).

2   Ben Shephard, *The Long Road Home: The Aftermath of the Second World War* (New York: Alfred A. Knopf, 2011), 121.

3   Ben Shephard, *After Daybreak: The Liberation of Bergen-Belsen, 1945* (New York: Schocken Books, 2005), 167.

4   Agate Nesaule, *A Woman in Amber: Healing the Trauma of War and Exile* (London: Penguin Books, 1995), 279.

5   *Par atgriesanos Dzimtene* [About Returning Home], March, June, and July 1957.

6   *Dzimtenes Balss* [Homeland Voice], January 1, 1959.

7   ITS (International Tracing Service), UNESCO, *Name: PLATACS, First Name: Marija*, November 10, 2015.

Chapter 12: Immigrants

1   "DP Camps Following World War II," http://www.geni.com/Displaced-Persons-Camp. (accessed November 10, 2015)

2   Andris Straumanis, "Significant Immigration Waves," *Latvian Americans*, http://www.everyculture.com/Latvian Americans. (accessed December 14, 2015)

3   "The Beginning of Displacement," Camps in Germany (1944-1951) for Refugees from Baltic Countries, http://www.archiv.org.lv/beginning of displacement. (accessed September 23, 2015)

4   "The Dispersal of Refugees," Camps in Germany (1944-1951) for Refugees from Baltic Countries, http://www.archiv.org.lv/the dispersal of refugees. (accessed September 23, 2015)

5   Tara Zahra, *The Lost Children: Reconstructing Europe's Families after World War II*, (Cambridge: Harvard University, 2011). Kindle ed., [Kindle locations 1278–1280; 1288–1289; 2832–2837]

6   Wikipedia, "Structure," *Universal Declaration of Human Rights*, last modified March 3, 2016, http://en.wikipedia.org/Universal Declaration of Human Rights.

7   Juris Prikulis, NATO Research Fellow, "Migration and Repatriation Issues in Post-Soviet Countries: The Latvian Case," Final Report, Democratic Institutions Fellowships Programme, Riga, June 1997, http://nato.int/acad/fellow/95-97/prikulis.pdf. (accessed November 2, 2015)

8   Jānis Riekstiņš, *Latvijas Bāreni, kuri pazaudeja savu dzimteni* [Latvian Orphans, Who are in Your Homeland], (Riga: Mansards, 2015), 93–96.

9   "Repatriation," Camps in Germany (1944-1951) for Refugees from Baltic Countries, accessed September 23, 2015, http://www.archiv. org.lv/repatriation. (accessed September 23, 2015)

10   Gitta Sereny, "Stolen Children: Interview with Gitta Sereny," *Talk*, 1999. http://jewishvirtuallibrary.org. (accessed November 10, 2015)

11   Jānis Riekstiņš, *Latvijas Bāreni*, Ibid.

12   A. Zvēriņš, "Fate of Latvian Orphans on the American Continent," *Latvia Amerikā*, July 2, 1955.

13   Ben Shephard, *The Long Road Home: The Aftermath of the Second World War* (New York: Alfred A. Knopf, 2011), 428.

14   E. Plūme, "For the sake of truth: How can we help orphans taken to USA and Canada?" *Latvija Amerikā* No. 41 (June 1, 1955).

15   The record for the final outcome of unaccompanied minors included the following: 6,871 were repatriated - mostly to Eastern Europe; 1,889 were resettled abroad - mostly Jewish children; 3,793 "disappeared" - including 2,400 Jewish children, to Palestine or Germany; 1,138 who were eighteen were released into the general population; and 1,073 were reunited with relatives in exile. Tara Zahra, Ibid. [Kindle locations 2828–2832].

16   Richard Solberg, *Open Doors: The Story of Lutherans Resettling Refugees* (St. Louis, Missouri: Concordia Publishing House, 1992), 14.

17   Ben Shephard, Ibid., 498, 501.

18   Richard Solberg, Ibid., 24, 34–36.

19   A. deCocatrix, Letter Re: PLATACE, Marija Inq.: Bronislav Platacis—father. May 2, 1961, Copy of 6.3.3.2/106373474 in conformity with its ITS Archives Bad Arolsen, Germany.

20   E. Plūme, Ibid.

21   Ben Shephard, Ibid, 509.

Chapter 13: Marija Platača's Life

1   This traditional Latvian folk song is best known as a musical composition by Jānis Cimze who composed it in 1872, which was performed in 1873 at the All-Latvian Singing Festival by a male

choir. The verses appear below. Wikipedia, "Lyrics," *Rīga dimd*, last modified March 2013, http://en.wikipedia.org/wiki/Rīga dimd.

> Rīga resounds, Rīga resounds
> Who made Rīga so resound?
> Aijaijā Tralalā
> Who made Rīga so resound?
>
> Those forging a dowry for that maiden
> The one with three ilk of brothers
> Aijaijā Tralalā
> The one with three ilk of brothers
>
> Brother to her father forged the dowry
> Brother to her mother forged the dowry
> Aijaijā Tralalā
> Brother to her mother forged the dowry
>
> True brother to herself
> Cast its lid of gold
> Aijaijā Tralalā
> Cast its lid of gold

2   The first postwar kolkhoz (collective farm) in Latvia was set up in November 1946. In May 1947, the Moscow Politburo called for the beginning of thorough collectivization. By early 1949, against the backdrop of a massive deportation of recalcitrants (perhaps one out of every ten farmers in Estonia and Latvia, along with their families) and confiscatory taxation, the move to collective farms became a stampede. Entire villages and townships joined. By the end of 1950, 226,900 farms had been organized into 11,776 collectives, an average of 127.7 farms per kolkhoz. By Stalin's death in 1953, the process was complete. Modris Eksteins *Walking Since Daybreak: A Story of Eastern Europe, World War II, and the Heart of Our Century*, (Boston: Houghton Mifflin Harcourt, 2000), Kindle ed., Kindle locations 1803–1807.

3   "Forests in Latvia," *Young People in European Forests The International Contest*, http://www.Ypef.eu/forest_lv. (accessed January 13, 2016)

4   Malcolm Margolin, "Felling a Tree," *Mother Earth News*, October/November 2005, http://www.motherearthnews.com/homesteading-and-livestok/felling-a-tree.aspx.

5   "About JVLMA," Jāzeps Vītols Latvian Academy of Music, last modified December 10, 2010, http://www.jvlma.lv/english.

6   "How to Milk a Cow by Hand with Videos and Images," http://countryfarm-lifestyles.com/how to milk a cow. (accessed January 4, 2016)

7   Monika Platace Millere, "Two Hundred Kilometers of a Cow," *Saskarsme* [Communication], November 9, 2009.

Chapter 14: Adoption

1   Tara Zahra, *The Lost Children: Reconstructing Europe's Families after World War II*, (Cambridge: Harvard University Press, March 2015), Kindle ed., [Kindle locations 3383–3384].

2   Ben Shephard, *The Long Road Home*: *The Aftermath of the Second World War* (New York: Alfred A. Knopf, 2011), 433.

3   Holly Case, "Innocents Lost: On Postwar Orphans," The Nation, *Culture*, October 12, 2011, http://www.thenation.com/Holly Case/ Innocents Lost: On Postwar Orphans. (accessed Decmeber 13, 2015)

4   A. Zvēirņš, "Fate of Latvian Orphans on the American Continent," *Latvija Amerikā* 51, July 2, 1955.

5   Ave Futchs, letter, April 1949, Jersey City, New Jersey.

6   Mary Winston directed the Displaced Persons Project for the National Lutheran Council. Her responsibilities included fielding questions from all over the church about the legislation pending in Congress. She also answered all inquiries from people interested in adopting refugee children. Richard W. Solberg, *Open Doors: The Story of Lutherans Resettling Refugees* (Concordia Publishing House, 1992), 35.

7   Tara Zahra, *The Lost Children*, Ibid. (Kindle locations 1271–1274).

8   Ibid.

9 Cenage Learning "Early Literature on Institutionalization," Orphans, http://www.encyclopedia.com/topic/orphanages. (accessed Jnuary 10, 2016)

10 Boris Gindis, Center for Cognitive-Developmental Asessment & Remediation,"Post-Orphanage Behavior in Internationally Adopted Children," April 2012, http://bgcenter.com/Post- Orphanage Behavior in Internationally Adopted Children. (accessed December 8, 2015)

11 H. Carl Haywood, ed., "Cognitive Language,and Educational Issues of Children Adopted from Overseas Orphanages," *Journal of Cognitive Education and Psychology* Vol. 4, No. 3, February, 2005, http:// bgcenter. com/Cognitive Language, and Educational Issues of Children Adopted from Overseas Orphanages. (accessed December 9, 2015)

12 "Asks Return of Refugee She Sheltered," *Harvey Tribune*, Harvey, Illinois, January 18, 1951.

Chapter 15: Return

1 Krasnoyarsk is a city and the administrative center of Krasnoyarsk, Russia, in the center of the country, located on the Yenisei River. It is the third-largest city in Siberia after Novosibirsk and Omsk, with a population of 1,035,528 as of the 2010 census. Wikipedia, "Krasnoyarsk," last modified February 26, 2016, http://en.wikipedia.org/Krasnoyarsk.

2 Ērgļi is a village in Ērgļi parish, Latvia. Ērgļi had 2,186 residents as of 2006. It is located in the center of Latvia, in the cultural region of Vidzeme. Wikipedia, "Ērgļi," last modified,October 26, 2015, http://en.wikipedia.org/ Ērgļi.

3 Conversation with brother Andris Platacis in Dobele, Latvia, August 9, 10, 2015.

4 Three of the leaders of the Soviet partisans—Otomars Oškalns, Imants Sudmalis, and Vilis Samsons—were awarded the title Hero of the Soviet Union. "Heroes of the Soviet Union," http:// www. pediaview.com/Soviet partisans. (accessed February 2, 2016)

Platacis Forebears

1   Family lore: phone conversations with Leonora Ķieģelis and email exchanges with Juris Sorokins, 2014-2015.

2   Family lore, Leonora Platace Ķieģelis, great granddaughter of Abrams Platacis.

3   The Russian Imperial Census of 1897 was the first and the only census carried out in the Russian Empire (Finland was excluded). It recorded demographic data as of January 28,1897. Previously, the Central Statistical Bureau issued statistical tables based on fiscal lists. The second Russian Census was scheduled for December 1915, but was cancelled because of the outbreak of World War I one and a half years earlier (in July 1914). The next census to take place in Russia occurred at the end of 1926, probably well after the death of Abrams Platacis. This assumes he was about 20 years of age in 1860, when his son, Silvestrs, was born. He therefore would have been 86 years old in 1826, which was well beyond the life expectancy of most persons at that time. Wikipedia, "Russian Empire Census," last modified January 4, 2016, http://en.wikipedia. Org/Russian Empire Census.

4   *Valsts Statistiskā Pārvalde* (National Statistical Administration), Ceturtā tautas skaitīšana 1935. Gada. 12. Februāri, (The Fourth People's Counting of 12 February 1935) Personas kartite (Personal card) for Silvestrs Platacis and Dominese Platacis.

5   The Pale was first established in 1791, when the White-Russian Jews, who had passed under Russian rule (1772) at the first partition of Poland, were forbidden to join merchant or artisan guilds in governments other than those of White Russia. It lasted until the fall of the Russian Empire in 1917. Herman Rosenthal, Jewish Encyclopedia, Pale of Settlement, http://www.jewishencyclopedia. com/Pale of Settlement. (accessed November 8, 2015)

6   The Pale of Settlement was a portion of Russia comprised about 20% of the territory of European Russia and largely corresponded to historical borders of the former Polish–Lithuanian Commonwealth and the Crimean Khanate. It included much of present-day Lithuania,

Belarus, Poland, Moldova, Latvia, Ukraine, and parts of western Russia. Wikipedia, "Latgale," last modified February 5, 2016.

7   Public Notice, "Rēzeknes aprinka Zemes Jericības Komitejai" (Rēzekne Land Committee), containing a request for a State Land Bank loan for Rusiski farm in the name of Silvestrs Platacis, son of Jgnata (a.k.a Ignats, Abrams), signed by son Kazimirs Platacis on January 27, 1931.

INDEX

T

Tērmanis, Herberts (a.k.a, Peteris Aigars), 99
Third Reich, 53, 57, 66, 69, 73, 84, 87, 92
typhoid, 54–55, 57, 63, 68–69, 72

U

Ulmanis, Karlis, 19, 194n5
United Nations Relief and Rehabilitation Administration (UNRRA), xi, 73, 129, 133, 139
Universal Declaration of Rights, 130, 133

V

Vītiņa, Zelma, 132
Vituma, Ilze, xiv–xv

W

Winston, Mary, 158, 213n5
Wolow filtration camp, 114

Y

Year of Terror, 27

Z

Zahra, Tara, 45, 130–31, 156, 159–60, 200